D1101259

The Prime Minister in
Canadian Government
and Politics

To Jennifer Louise

The Prime Minister in Canadian Government and Politics

R. M. Punnett

Canadian Controversies Series

Macmillan of Canada
Maclean-Hunter Press

Canadian Cataloguing in Publication Data

Punnett, R. M., 1936-
  The Prime Minister in Canadian government and politics

(Canadian controversies series)

Includes bibliographical references and index.
ISBN 0-7705-1492-8 bd.   ISBN 0-7705-1493-6 pa.

1. Prime ministers — Canada.   2. Canada — Politics and government — 1867-   I. Title.   II. Series.

JL99.P85   354′.71′0313   C77-001039-3

Printed in Canada for

The Macmillan Company of Canada Limited
70 Bond Street
Toronto M5B 1X3

Contents

Canadian Controversies Series

Canadian political commentators have adopted the full range of political styles, from cold detachment to partisan advocacy. The Canadian Controversies Series is disciplined by the idea that while political analysis must be based on sound descriptive and explanatory modes of thought, social scientists should not abnegate the role of evaluating political systems. Such evaluations require a conscious approach to the interrelationships between facts and values, empirical and normative considerations in politics.

Each theme in the series has been chosen to illustrate some basic principles of Canadian political life and to allow the respective authors freedom to develop normative positions on the related problems. It is hoped that the volumes will stimulate debate and advance public understanding of some of the major questions which confront the Canadian political system. By treating the enduring themes and problems in Canada, the authors will also illustrate the important contribution that social science can offer to politics in terms of facts, ideas, theories and comparative frameworks within which meaningful controversy can take place. Creative political thought must not be divorced from the political fabric of a country but form an integral part of it.

ROBERT J. JACKSON,
General Editor

Preface

I wish to thank a number of people for their advice and assistance in the preparation of this monograph. I am particularly grateful to the editor of the Canadian Controversies Series, Robert J. Jackson, for initiating the project and for providing guidance throughout the various stages of its production. I am also greatly indebted to J. R. Mallory and B. W. Headey, who both read an early draft of the manuscript; to J. C. Courtney, who read a later draft; and to numerous other colleagues in Canada and Britain who responded to my many requests for advice and information. My thanks go to McMaster University and Strathclyde University for providing me with secretarial assistance, and to Macmillan of Canada (especially Beverley Beetham and Virgil Duff) for their efficient processing of my manuscript.

Finally, and above all, I am grateful to my wife, Marjory, for undertaking much of the typing and for sustaining me at all times, and to my daughters, Jennifer and Alison, for allowing me some free time in which to write.

R. M. PUNNETT
Hamilton, Ontario
1976

List of Tables

1.   Introduction

Two distinct themes can be detected in much of the literature on Canadian government and politics of the last ten years or so. The first theme is that more and more power is passing into the hands of the Prime Minister of the day: far from being characterized as a "parliamentary system", or a "cabinet system", Canadian government and politics is above all else "prime-ministerial" or "presidential" in character. Professor F. F. Schindeler,[1] for example, has argued that the Canadian system has evolved from a nineteenth-century "Cabinet model", in which power rested firmly with the Cabinet as a whole, through an early-nineteenth-century "bureaucratic model", in which the Cabinet became subordinate to the civil service, to a modern "prime-ministerial model" in which the Prime Minister is supreme. Schindeler claims:

> . . . the Prime Minister occupies a position of power in some ways unrivalled even by the President of the United States. We may call it parliamentary government or cabinet government but in fact we have prime-ministerial government in Canada.[2]

Schindeler points to the importance of the Prime Minister's electoral role, and the influence over ministers and back-benchers that comes from his powers of patronage. He emphasizes particularly, however, the resources that are available to the Prime Minister in the Privy Council Office and the Prime Minister's Office, noting that these expanding institutions provide the Prime Minister with a private bureaucracy. They are an invaluable supplement to civil-service and ministerial sources of advice and information, and allow the Prime Minister to develop alternative policies to those emerging from the departments of state.

Similarly, Professor Denis Smith, in an influential and much quoted paper presented to the Priorities for Canada Conference in 1969,[3] argued that Canadian Prime Ministers have increased their power, and Parliament has lost much of its authority, so that . . . "we seem to have created in Canada a presidential system without its congressional advantages."[4]

The first strand of Professor Smith's argument is that the Prime Minister dominates his Cabinet, the bureaucracy, Parliament, and his party in and out of Parliament. The selection of party leaders by grass-roots delegates at leadership Conventions, rather than by caucus or by the Cabinet; the consequent difficulties involved in replacing an established Prime Minister; the Prime Minister's control over the timing of elections; the extent to which elections, when they are held, are competitions between party leaders; the tendency for the public to see the government as "one man's government"—these several factors, Professor Smith claims, give the Prime Minister overwhelming authority within the Canadian political system.

The second strand of his argument is that Parliament, in direct contrast to the Prime Minister, is chronically short of both prestige and power. It is ill-equipped to scrutinize financial or highly technical measures, or to digest the volume of legislation that has emerged in an age of expanded government activities. The strength of party discipline, and the procedural rules that enable the government to overcome parliamentary obstruction, mean that Parliament has little real influence over the content of legislation. What is more, the much heralded parliamentary reforms under Pearson and Trudeau *reduced* Parliament's power by adding to the government's procedural armoury. Smith sees the result as a situation in which the Prime Minister dominates his ministerial colleagues, enjoys considerable security of tenure, and faces little real threat to his policies in the legislature.

Some support for Smith's views on parliamentary impotence comes from Robert J. Jackson and Michael M. Atkinson in their analysis of the Canadian legislative system.[5] Jackson and Atkinson argue that the balance of power between Parliament and the executive needs to be adjusted. Backbenchers, they claim, tend to support the government blindly, the Opposition is inadequate as an alternative government, and rather than using MPs to establish links with the electorate, the Prime

Minister tends to use Royal Commissions, task forces, and public opinion polls. Thus, say Jackson and Atkinson:

> . . . the executive too often assumes a posture of complacency toward the legislature. In part this is attributable to Parliament's inability to hold the executive responsible for the ever-increasing scope of government activities, to control the commitments made at federal-provincial conferences and to compete with the personalized politics of the Prime Minister.[6]

Many other writers, while not necessarily accepting the "prime-ministerial power" interpretation of Canadian government, nevertheless have underlined important features of a Prime Minister's power and influence. Many electoral studies, for example, have emphasized the importance of the leader's role in attracting votes to his party. Peter Regenstreif, in *The Diefenbaker Interlude*,[7] used survey evidence to show the importance of John Diefenbaker's contribution to the campaigns that he fought as Conservative Party leader. Regenstreif concluded that:

> The personality orientation of Canadian parties is a functional ingredient of a political system in which social reference affiliations are weak mediators of political loyalties.[8]

John Meisel, in his study of the 1968 election,[9] also produced survey evidence to illustrate the extent of the leader's role in determining electoral behaviour:

> Looking at Canada as a whole, . . . we find that the leader was the most important factor, among those suggested, in the voting decision. He was followed by the party taken generally, the candidates and, a long distance behind, the work of the elected Members in the previous Parliament.[10]

Thomas A. Hockin has pointed to the Prime Minister's unique role as a public persuader:

> His power to command national attention both during and between elections, if not absolute, is usually more potent than that of any other political leader in Canada and there are times when his words are greeted with an unusual amount of emotional intensity.[11]

Again, John C. Courtney, in his analysis of the selection of national party leaders,[12] points out that it is much easier for a leader selected by a Convention than for a leader selected by caucus to "place himself above his Cabinet colleagues".[13] He warns that as a result of the personalization of politics through the Convention system "Canadians now run the risk of fostering a plebiscitory mentality with respect to Canadian politics."[14]

J. R. Mallory, in reviewing the relations between the Prime Minister and his ministers, underlines the many rights that the Prime Minister alone enjoys:

> It is he who advises the Sovereign on the appointment of the Governor General. He, and only he, can advise a Governor General to appoint a minister or to accept his resignation. By resigning himself, a Prime Minister brings his ministry to an end. His right to advise on the dissolution of Parliament is a threat which he can hold over his colleagues and followers, for no politician welcomes the trouble and expense of fighting an election. He possesses the undoubted right to issue orders in any department without consulting the minister, and he may assume the administration of a department himself. . . . Finally, only the Prime Minister can advise the Governor General that the normal secrecy surrounding the Crown's confidential business may be relaxed.[15]

Comments such as these in standard works on Canadian government and politics provide ammunition for those who claim that the Canadian system is preponderantly prime-ministerial in character.

A second related theme in recent Canadian political literature is that those who have held the office of Prime Minister in recent years have been deficient in the arts of government. Best-selling books by political journalists have produced uniformly critical judgments of the reigns of John Diefenbaker, Lester Pearson, and Pierre Trudeau. Peter C. Newman's judgment on John Diefenbaker, in *Renegade in Power*, was that:

> He gave the people a leadership cult, without leadership . . . despite a lifetime spent in trying furiously to become prime minister of Canada, the man from Prince Albert had not the least inkling of what he wanted to do when he achieved that high office, and was rendered impotent by the magnitude of the claim it places upon its incumbent.[16]

Equally Lester Pearson's premiership is likened by Newman, in *The Distemper of Our Times*, to:

. . . the voyage of some peeling, once-proud, now leaky excursion steamer, lurching from port to port, with the captain making up the schedule as he went along, too busy keeping afloat to spend much time on the bridge . . . .[17]

Trudeau's reign as Prime Minister, according to Walter Stewart in *Shrug*, has been characterized by: ". . . confrontation, division, autocracy and the beginnings of the end of parliamentary democracy".[18]

Collectively these three judgments suggest that Canadians have been very badly let down by their recent Prime Ministers. In conjunction with the first theme, the judgments provide an extremely gloomy picture of modern Canadian government and politics—more and more power is passing into the hands of Prime Ministers who, as individuals, lack the talent to use it effectively. Is this a fair interpretation of the situation? Almost certainly it is not, and in this book an attempt will be made to redress the balance. Three main arguments will be presented:

1) The roles that the Prime Minister has to perform, and the skills that he is required to possess, are much more numerous than critics generally allow.

2) There are particular features of the Canadian political system that focus public attention on the Prime Minister and build up public expectations of what he personally can achieve—with perhaps the clearest examples of this being the almost Messianic powers attributed to John Diefenbaker and Pierre Trudeau when they first became Prime Minister.

3) The practical limitations upon what a Prime Minister *can* achieve are considerable, so that there is an almost inevitable gap between expectations and fulfilment.

The book is not intended to be an *apologia* for Pierre Trudeau or his recent predecessors. Rather, it is an attempt to assess the practical realities of the Prime Minister's roles and power in Canadian government and politics. To this end the next chapter examines the characteristics of those who have held the post of Prime Minister of Canada, and the stages that make up a Prime Minister's life-cycle. These several stages are then examined in turn. Chapter Three looks at the process by which a Prime Minister acquires the post, with particular emphasis on the factors that contribute to the personalization of Canadian politics. Chapter Four deals with the restraints upon the Prime Minister's freedom to select ministers and devise decision-making machinery, and Chapter Five highlights the difficulties he faces in leading his government in its deliberations. Chapter Six deals with the Prime Minister and Parliament. In Chapter Seven the analysis comes full circle with a look at the process of retaining office. First of all, however, the men and the job.

NOTES

1. In T. A. Hockin, ed., *The Apex of Power* (Scarborough: Prentice-Hall, 1971), pp. 22-48.
2. Ibid., p. 48.
3. Denis Smith, "President and Parliament", paper presented to the *Priorities for Canada Conference*, Niagara Falls, October 1969.
4. Ibid., p. 12.
5. Robert J. Jackson and Michael M. Atkinson, *The Canadian Legislative System* (Toronto: Macmillan, 1974).
6. Ibid., p. 7.
7. Peter Regenstreif, *The Diefenbaker Interlude* (Toronto: Longmans, 1965).
8. Ibid., p. 24.
9. John Meisel, *Working Papers on Canadian Politics* (Montreal: McGill-Queen's University Press, 1972), p. 31.
10. Ibid., p. 31.
11. Hockin, *Apex of Power*, p. 18.
12. John C. Courtney, *The Selection of National Party Leaders in Canada* (Toronto: Macmillan, 1973).
13. Ibid., p. 225.
14. Ibid., p. 225.
15. J. R. Mallory, *The Structure of Canadian Government* (Toronto: Macmillan, 1971), pp. 85-6.
16. Peter C. Newman, *Renegade in Power* (Toronto: McClelland and Stewart, 1963), pp. xi-xiii.
17. Peter C. Newman, *The Distemper of Our Times* (Toronto: McClelland and Stewart, 1968), p. xii.
18. Walter Stewart, *Shrug* (Toronto: New Press, 1972), p. 1.

2.   The Men
       and the Job

The powers and duties of the Prime Minister of Canada are
not enshrined in any statute, and the office carries virtually
no legal authority. The Prime Minister's powers are exercised
through the Governor General, the Privy Council, and the
ministers of the Crown. The essence of the Prime Minister's
position is his ability to carry out the task of forming and
leading a government. His authority rests on four main pillars.

1) He is the elected leader of his party, and normally will
   have received public endorsement at a general election. A
   Prime Minister, of course, may take up the post in mid-
   Parliament, and then (like Arthur Meighen, on two occasions, and Sir Charles Tupper) lose the election at the end
   of it, or (like Sir John Abbott, Sir John Thompson, and Sir
   Mackenzie Bowell) surrender the post before the election.
   Most Prime Ministers, however, receive electoral approval
   at some stage—and very often are major contributors to
   their party's victory at the polls.

2) Once he is invited to form a government he acquires vast
   powers of patronage, not only with Cabinet positions, but
   also with appointments to his private staff, the Senate, the
   bureaucracy, other regulatory agencies, and the judiciary.

3) Having appointed his ministers, he is the political head of
   the government. He is chairman of the Cabinet, and chief
   co-ordinator of the work of government. Even within the
   doctrine of collective ministerial responsibility, and within
   a federal Constitution, the Prime Minister is seen to be
   the individual *principally* responsible for the government
   of the state.

4) He is the person to whom his party colleagues primarily

look to provide a link with the electorate, and to secure the government's retention of office by explaining and defending its record before Parliament, the party, the press, pressure groups, and the public.

These four pillars of a Prime Minister's authority represent distinct stages in a prime-ministerial life-cycle. Later in the chapter this life-cycle will be looked at in more detail. First of all, however, it is necessary to look at the background and prior experience of those who have held the post of Prime Minister of Canada.

FIFTEEN PRIME MINISTERS

a. Social Background

Canada has had fifteen Prime Ministers since 1867 (see Table 2:1). Do they have any common characteristics in terms of background and career patterns? The premiership is an "old man's occupation" in that the Prime Ministers were, on the average, 58 when they acquired the job and 67 when they left it (see Table 2:2). There have been wide variations around these average figures, of course, from Tupper, who was 74 when he got the job, to Meighen who was 46. Mackenzie King and Trudeau were also in their forties when they were appointed. Nevertheless, seven of the fifteen were in their sixties or seventies when appointed, ten held the post beyond the age of 65 (the normal retirement age in other jobs), and eight reached their seventieth year while in office. Macdonald was 76 when he died in office (while his British contemporary, Gladstone, was 89). Today, however, it would be much less practical for such old men to hold the job. Television coverage exposes senility, and now, in an age of big government, nuclear confrontation, and summit diplomacy, the Prime Minister's role is a much more exacting one than was the case in the past.

The regional background of Prime Ministers is important in a federal country with distinct regional identities and tensions. There are two main considerations here. In the first place, it is desirable that justice be seen to be done, in that if Ontario monopolized the premiership it would add to the regional claims that Canada is an unbalanced, Toronto-

Table 2:1

PRIME MINISTERS OF CANADA

Prime Minister	Party	Tenure
Sir John A. Macdonald	Lib–Con	July 1st, 1867 — Nov. 5th, 1873
Alexander Mackenzie	Lib	Nov. 5th, 1873 — Oct. 9th, 1878
Sir John A. Macdonald	Con	Oct. 9th, 1878 — June 6th, 1891
Sir John Abbott	Con	June 15th, 1891 — Nov. 24th, 1892
Sir John Thompson	Con	Nov. 25th, 1892 — Dec. 12th, 1894
Sir Mackenzie Bowell	Con	Dec. 13th, 1894 — April 27th, 1896
Sir Charles Tupper	Con	April 27th, 1896 — July 8th, 1896
Sir Wilfrid Laurier	Lib	July 9th, 1896 — Oct. 6th, 1911
Sir Robert Borden	Con	Oct. 7th, 1911 — July 10th, 1920
Arthur Meighen	Con	July 10th, 1920 — Dec. 29th, 1921
W. L. Mackenzie King	Lib	Dec. 29th, 1921 — June 28th, 1926
Arthur Meighen	Con	June 28th, 1926 — Sept. 25th, 1926
W. L. Mackenzie King	Lib	Sept. 25th, 1926 — Aug. 7th, 1930
R. B. Bennett	Con	Aug. 7th, 1930 — Oct. 23rd, 1935
W. L. Mackenzie King	Lib	Oct. 23rd, 1935 — Nov. 15th, 1948
Louis St. Laurent	Lib	Nov. 15th, 1948 — June 21st, 1957
John Diefenbaker	Con	June 21st, 1957 — April 22nd, 1963
Lester B. Pearson	Lib	April 22nd, 1963 — April 20th, 1968
Pierre Elliott Trudeau	Lib	April 20th, 1968 —

SOURCE: Government of Canada, *Guide to Canadian Ministries Since Confederation 1867-1957* (and Supplement 1957-67), (Ottawa: Public Archives of Canada, 1957 and 1967).

Table 2:2

SOCIAL BACKGROUND OF PRIME MINISTERS

Prime Minister	Province		Age as PM	Religion	Occupation
	Birth	Adult Life			
Macdonald	(Britain)	Ontario	52–76	Presbyterian	Law
Mackenzie	(Britain)	Ontario	51–56	Baptist	Journalist/Stonemason
Abbott	Quebec	Quebec	70	Anglican	Law/Lecturer
Thompson	Nova Scotia	Nova Scotia	48–50	Catholic	Law/Lecturer
Bowell	(Britain)	Ontario	70–72	Methodist	Journalist
Tupper	Nova Scotia	Nova Scotia	74	Anglican	Doctor
Laurier	Quebec	Quebec	54–69	Catholic	Law
Borden	Nova Scotia	Nova Scotia	57–65	Anglican	Law
Meighen	Ontario	Manitoba	46–52	Presbyterian	Law/Business
King	Ontario	Ontario	47–73	Presbyterian	Civil Service
Bennett	New Brunswick	Alberta	60–65	United Church	Law/Business
St. Laurent	Quebec	Quebec	66–75	Catholic	Law
Diefenbaker	Ontario	Saskatchewan	61–67	Baptist	Law
Pearson	Ontario	Ontario	65–70	United Church	Civil Service
Trudeau	Quebec	Quebec	48–	Catholic	Law/Lecturer

SOURCE: Biographical data from J. K. Johnson, ed., *The Canadian Directory of Parliament* (Ottawa: Public Archives of Canada, 1968).

dominated federation. More than this, however, a region *does* generally receive some practical advantage from having a local boy as Prime Minister. Three of the early Prime Ministers (Macdonald, Mackenzie, and Bowell) were born in Britain, and none of the Prime Ministers in the first fifty years of Confederation was born west of Montreal. Taking all fifteen Prime Ministers, none was born west of Ontario, but Meighen, Diefenbaker (both born in Ontario), and Bennett (born in New Brunswick) subsequently moved to the Prairies. Thus in terms of their provincial base during adult life, the regional distribution has been three Maritimers, four Quebeckers, five Ontarians, and three westerners—a distribution that corresponds remarkably closely to the present-day spread of population across Canada, and seems to contradict the assumption that at the summit Canadian politics is dominated by the provinces of Ontario and Quebec. These two provinces, however, have produced the longest serving Prime Ministers, so that in terms of the total number of years that a region has held the premiership, the distribution is: Maritimes, 10 years; Quebec, 31; Ontario, 52; and the west, 12. British Columbia, Prince Edward Island, and Newfoundland have yet to produce a Prime Minister. Nova Scotia, on the other hand, has clearly been over-represented with three, although all three attained office before the First World War when Nova Scotia made up a greater proportion of the total population than it does now.

This is not to say, of course, that there is a conscious attempt by each party to share its Prime Ministers, over time, among the provinces strictly according to population. Even if a party wished to draw its leaders from each province in turn, the established practice of selecting the party leader at a national Convention would make this very difficult to achieve. Conventions can be influenced, but not manipulated to quite such an extent. Rather, the rough regional balance that has been achieved is a consequence of each party's regional biases complementing each other. All six Liberal Prime Ministers have been drawn from Ontario or Quebec. The Conservatives, on the other hand, have had a broader spread, with three from Nova Scotia, two from Ontario, and one each from Quebec, Saskatchewan, Manitoba, and Alberta. All the Conservative Prime

Ministers in this century have had Maritime or Prairie bases. This distribution confirms the image of the Liberals as the party of central Canada, and of the Conservatives as the peripheral party.

Of the Prime Ministers from Quebec, one (Abbott) was an English-speaking Conservative Protestant, so that French Canadians, with just three Prime Ministers, have been slightly under-represented in relation to their proportion of the total population. Since the 1880s Liberal Party leaders have been drawn alternately from English Canada (Blake 1880, King 1919, Pearson 1958) and French Canada (Laurier 1887, St. Laurent 1948, Trudeau 1968). Whether this is now a firmly established principle of Liberal Party politics remains, however, a matter of speculation. Certainly, with the Convention system of selecting leaders, such alternation cannot be guaranteed. In a poll of delegates conducted before the 1968 Liberal Convention, for example, 60 per cent of the sample felt that there was now a party "tradition" of alternating between English-speaking and French-speaking leaders, but only 29 per cent felt that this was a good tradition. In the event, a majority of delegates voted for English-speaking candidates in every ballot except the last. Even in the final ballot Trudeau got only a bare majority, with 51 per cent of the votes against 49 per cent divided between the two English-speaking candidates.

The three French Canadians (Laurier, St. Laurent, and Trudeau), plus Thompson, are the only Catholics to have been Prime Minister, despite the fact that the Canadian population has normally been 40 to 50 per cent Catholic. Sir John Thompson, a convert to the faith, has been the only Catholic Conservative Prime Minister, while the Liberals have had three Catholics and three Protestants—illustrating yet again the Liberals' happy ability, over a period of time, to balance within their ranks Canada's regional, religious, and ethnic divisions.

The Prime Ministers have been highly untypical of the occupational and educational patterns of Canadians as a whole, in that most were lawyers before entering politics, and most were university graduates. Macdonald, Mackenzie, Thompson, Bowell, and Borden had little by way of formal education, but all the others, including all those appointed since the First

World War, attended university. There has been no equivalent, however, of the Oxford and Cambridge dominance of the British premiership, in that the Canadian graduates were spread among seven universities. Seven of the graduates took law degrees and subsequently practiced law, and three of the non-graduates also became lawyers. Thus two-thirds of the Prime Ministers had a legal background, and the others all came from middle-class professions (journalism, university teaching, and the civil service). Mackenzie was the closest to being a "working man", with his own stone-mason's business (Goldwin Smith's cruel verdict on him being that he "had been bred a stone-mason and as a premier a stone-mason he remained").[1] Even Mackenzie, however, had experience as a journalist, succeeding George Brown as editor of *The Globe*.

Thus, as former lawyers, teachers, and journalists, the majority of Prime Ministers were experienced in the art of communication, and particularly oral communication. Such skills are essential for a Prime Minister as for any politician. Alexander Brady saw lawyers as a substitute in Canada for a ruling class, in that they have the oral skills required for a parliamentary career, and, in contrast with most occupations, they can combine their parliamentary and professional roles.[2] It can be argued, however, that legal training is a bad preparation for the premiership, in that law is based essentially on precedent, whereas "leadership" requires innovation and the delegation of tasks to others. Peter Newman argues, for example, that Diefenbaker was skilled in the lawyer's art of public pleading, but, also as a result of his legal background, was cautious and indecisive.[3] Some of the lawyers blended their legal training with other experience: two also became businessmen and three taught at universities. Bennett was a lawyer who became very successful in business, and brought his boardroom skills with him into the Cabinet. Of other professional skills, Mackenzie King's experience as a conciliator as Deputy Minister of Labour and then as an industrial consultant, was no doubt useful training for the task of coaxing agreement from Cabinet ministers and provincial leaders. Similarly, Lester Pearson's diplomatic training, and particularly his experience at the United Nations, was perhaps a valuable preparation for the politics of compromise that were required throughout the lifetime of his minority government.

b. *Parliamentary and Ministerial Careers*

When Trudeau became Prime Minister in 1968 much was made of the fact that he had behind him less than three years of parliamentary experience, and one year of Cabinet experience. In this how different was Trudeau from his predecessors, and was his lack of experience important? Trudeau certainly had less parliamentary experience than any of his predecessors, but Mackenzie King and St. Laurent were not very far ahead of him (see Table 2:3). There are distinct differences between the two parties in this. All nine Conservative Prime Ministers have been "parliamentarians" in that at the time of their appointment they had ten or more years of legislative experience at the federal or provincial levels. Tupper had a total of 30 years, Abbott 27, and Bowell 24. Of the six Liberal Prime Ministers, Mackenzie, Laurier, and Pearson had more than ten years legislative experience when they became Premier (with Laurier having twenty-five), but St. Laurent had only seven, Mackenzie King, six, and Trudeau, a mere two and a half years. The average for the Liberals was just under ten years, compared with double that for the Conservatives. John Bracken, George Drew, and Robert Stanfield, who led the Conservatives only in Opposition, also fit into this pattern with, respectively, 20, 10, and 18 years of provincial legislative experience before becoming federal leaders.

Prime Ministers appointed in the first fifty years of Confederation had considerably more legislative experience than those appointed since 1917, with this being true of both parties (see Table 2:4). This temporal division more or less coincides with the change to the Convention method of selecting party leaders. Experienced parliamentarians have often been overlooked at Conventions, and in fact at only three of the eleven Liberal and Conservative leadership conventions has the candidate with most parliamentary experience been selected. There are other factors, however, that contribute to the Prime Minister's comparative lack of legislative experience. In Canada

Table 2:3

RANGE OF PRIOR LEGISLATIVE AND
EXECUTIVE EXPERIENCE OF PRIME MINISTERS

| | Legislative | | Executive | | | |
	Federal (Years)	Provincial (Years)	Federal (Posts)	Federal (Years)	Provincial (Posts)	Provincial (Years)
Macdonald		23			5	12
Mackenzie	6	7			1	1
Abbott	17¼	10	1	4	1	1
Thompson	7¼	4½	2	7¼	2	3¾
Bowell	27		4	16¼		
Tupper	18	12	7	10¼	2	7
Laurier	22	3	1	1		
Borden	15					
Meighen	12		4	7		
King	5½		1	2¼		
Bennett	11	8	6*	½		
St. Laurent	7		3	6½		
Diefenbaker	16¾					
Pearson	14½		1	8¾		
Trudeau	2½		1	1		

*Bennett held five posts simultaneously in Meighen's short-lived "Caretaker" Ministry in 1926.

SOURCE: J. K. Johnson, ed., *The Canadian Directory of Parliament* (Ottawa: Public Archives of Canada, 1968).

Table 2:4

PRIOR LEGISLATIVE EXPERIENCE OF PRIME MINISTERS

| | Average Number of Years of Legislative Experience | | |
PMS Appointed	Lib	Con	All
1867-1917	19	22	21
1919-1968	7½	16	13

SOURCE: J. K. Johnson, ed., *The Canadian Directory of Parliament* (Ottawa: Public Archives of Canada, 1968).

the high turnover rate among MPs means that there are comparatively few long-serving MPs anyway. It also means that it is relatively easy, and acceptable, to co-opt "outsiders" to serve as party leaders. Provincial politics provides a ready source of talent outside Ottawa. In the nineteenth century Tupper and Thompson graduated from careers as provincial premiers to the federal premiership, and in this century Bracken, Drew, and Stanfield have tried to follow suit, although without reaching the premiership. The Liberal Party traditionally has turned to those who have had careers in the public service (King and Pearson) or were active in Quebec provincial politics (St. Laurent and Trudeau).

A degree of parliamentary experience might be expected to be beneficial to a potential Prime Minister. As Prime Minister he will have to appear regularly in Parliament to explain and defend government policies, and prior service will enable him to get the feel of the House and learn its rules (the informal and unofficial rules as well as the procedural ones). As Lester Pearson expressed it:

> . . . it is a great help to have had a long parliamentary experience; to have risen from the ranks in Parliament where you can acquire, if you have not had it instinctively, a feeling for Parliament, of its importance and traditions.[4]

Pearson himself, however, has been criticized for not attending Parliament frequently enough, and for losing touch with the "moods" of the House and the caucus.[5] Trudeau's often gauche behaviour in the House, particularly in the 1968-72 Parliament, was sometimes attributed to his lack of legislative service.

Legislative service, however, can take many forms. Experience gained at the provincial level can supplement federal parliamentary experience, and can help a Prime Minister to appreciate both parts of the federal-provincial relationship. Service on the backbenches enables the Prime Minister to observe caucus machinery in operation, and experience party discipline. Liberal prime ministers, in particular, have been short of this specifically backbench experience. Legislative experience while the party is in Opposition enables the potential Prime Minister to experience the other side of the parliamentary battle. Subsequently, as Prime Minister he will enjoy the advantages of being a "poacher turned gamekeeper". It is possible, of course, that too long a spell in Opposition will result in the Prime Minister being incurably "Opposition minded". This accusation was often levelled at John Diefenbaker, whose seventeen years in Parliament before gaining the premiership were all spent in Opposition. A successful transition to office, after long years in Opposition, can be made, however, as was demonstrated by Borden (fifteen years in Opposition) and Laurier (nine years).

Of all the different forms of prior experience, however, service in the Cabinet might be expected to be the most useful for an aspiring Prime Minister. This will give him experience of Cabinet machinery and procedures, and of minister-Prime Minister relations. It will enable him to observe at close hand another Prime Minister at work, and learn from the way he handles Cabinet meetings, resolves conflicts, and organizes his time. As head of a department, he will become acquainted with civil-service attitudes and with the difficulties of dealing with complex policy issues through the medium of a large bureaucracy. Eleven of the fifteen Prime Ministers had some prior experience in the federal Cabinet, while Macdonald and Mackenzie had provincial Cabinet experience (Macdonald's experience, of course, inevitably being confined to the Province of Canada). Only Borden and Diefenbaker were completely without Cabinet experience.

The posts of Minister of Justice and Minister of External Affairs have been the most likely to lead on to the premiership. Trudeau, St. Laurent, and Thompson served as Minister of Justice immediately prior to becoming Prime Minister, and Bennett held the post earlier in his career. St. Laurent and Pearson held the post of Minister of External Affairs (and it is only since 1948 that this post has been held by anyone other than the Prime Minister himself). In contrast, the key Cabinet post of Minister of Finance has not proved to be a training ground for the premiership. Tupper and Bennett did hold this post, but for a total of less than eighteen months between them.

In general, the extent and variety of Prime Ministers' prior federal Cabinet experience has not been great. If Bowell and

Tupper (and, of course, Macdonald) are excluded, the average for the rest is just two years prior Cabinet experience, with only Thompson, Bennett, St. Laurent and Meighen holding more than one post. Even the addition of provincial Cabinet experience does not change the picture very much. Macdonald spent twelve years as a minister in the Province of Canada, Thompson and Tupper served as Premiers of Nova Scotia, and Mackenzie and Abbott spent a year in the Cabinets of Ontario and Quebec respectively, but none of the others had any provincial Cabinet experience. There has not been, then, any great transfer of provincial Premiers into the federal premiership, although the Conservatives while in Opposition have been led by no less than three former provincial premiers over the last forty years (Bracken of Manitoba, Drew of Ontario, and Stanfield of Nova Scotia).

Sir John A. Macdonald provides an example of a career in which a wide variety of ministerial and parliamentary experience proved to be a prelude to a long and distinguished premiership. There is certainly no necessary correlation, however, between the extent of prior Cabinet or parliamentary experience, and the subsequent degree of success as Prime Minister. Some of those with the greatest amount of prior experience have been the least memorable Prime Ministers. Of all fifteen Prime Ministers, Tupper had the greatest amount of Cabinet experience, serving ten years in the federal Cabinet and seven in provincial Cabinets, and holding nine different posts in all, including that of Premier of Nova Scotia. He was Prime Minister of Canada for just over two months, however, losing the 1896 election and failing again at the 1902 election as Leader of the Opposition. His tragedy was that he came to the premiership too late: he was passed over in 1892 and 1894, and by 1896 he was 74 years old and the Conservative Party fortunes were on the decline. Similarly Bowell had considerable ministerial experience, serving for sixteen years in four different posts. He lasted as Prime Minister for less than two years, however, before being overthrown by a Cabinet revolt.[6] Arthur Meighen had experience in four Cabinet posts, but his two spells as Prime Minister amounted to less than two years in all.

At the other extreme, Borden had no prior Cabinet experience at either the federal or provincial levels, and Laurier and Mackenzie King had only limited ministerial experience, but they became three of the four longest serving Canadian Prime Ministers. Trudeau, with only one year as a Cabinet minister, and less than three years in Parliament, has survived to become one of the longer serving Prime Ministers. Clearly, despite the advantages (referred to above) that are enjoyed by a Prime Minister who has had wide ministerial experience, there are clear compensations for a Prime Minister who has not had this. He has all the advantages of the layman over the expert. He is not conditioned to accept time-honoured practices and attitudes, and is not associated with past failures and established policies. He can thus present himself to the party and the public as the symbol of something new, and he can innovate more readily. What is more, the disadvantages of being a new boy in Parliament are minimized by the fact that the parliamentary turnover rate is so high that in most Parliaments there are relatively few long-serving MPs.

THE PRIME-MINISTERIAL LIFE-CYCLE

The stages in the prime-ministerial life-cycle were referred to at the beginning of the chapter. In more detail, what is involved at each stage of the cycle, and what particular skills does the Prime Minister have to possess for each process?

a. Acquiring the Post

This process itself involves three stages. The aspiring Prime Minister must first of all become party leader. The particular skills required for this task will vary with the method of selection that the party uses, be it selection by an elite group, by caucus, or by a Convention that is open to the various levels of the party. Both the main Canadian parties now use Conventions to select their leaders, and success at a Convention requires the ability to attract the support of grass-roots delegates drawn from across Canada. For this the aspiring Prime Minister requires the skills of the faction leader, so that he may pose convincingly as the embodiment of party interests. Having become party leader he has then to lead the party to victory in a general election. If, of course, he becomes Prime Minister in mid-Parliament, and retains the post for only a short time (as did Abbott, Thompson, and Bowell in the 1890s), he may not face the electorate at all. In order to hold the post for any length of time, however, he has to be able to win elections. For this task he is still a partisan figure, leading a political party, but he must also have the vote-catching skills to attract non-committed voters as well as the party faithful. Once the election has been won he has to move a stage further away from partisanship in order that he may exercise political and symbolic leadership over the nation as a whole. For this he has to be able to pose as the symbol of national interests and aspirations.

b. Forming a Government

The second stage in the cycle is the formation of a government. This involves the selection of teams of ministers and of advisers for the Prime Minister's personal staff, and also the creation of an organizational structure in which they can operate. For the selection of personnel, the Prime Minister requires the skills of the recruiting officer. He has to be able to find the right men, and then persuade them to serve together, under him, in the posts he wishes them to fill. In Australia and New Zealand members of the Cabinet are elected by caucus, and the Prime Minister merely appoints them to particular posts. The Canadian Prime Minister does not face this restriction on his freedom of choice, but nevertheless, the practical limitations upon his choice are considerable.

For the creation of satisfactory policy making and decision-taking machinery the Prime Minister requires the skills of the organization man. He inherits from his predecessor, of course, an on-going structure, and he is free to adapt it or leave it unchanged. At the macro-level of basic constitutional machinery, few changes have been made since Confederation, and the Canadian Constitution remains monarchical, federal, and parliamentary. At the micro-level, however, things have been much more fluid, with Prime Ministers making numerous changes over the years in matters such as the size of the Cabinet, the number and functions of its committees, the number of departments, and the size and functions of the Prime Minister's Office and the Privy Council Office.

c. *Leading the Government*

Having formed a government the Prime Minister then has to ensure that it operates effectively. This involves preserving its unity, controlling its output, and, on many occasions, representing it in negotiations with other governments and bodies at home and abroad. The most basic requirement is for the Prime Minister to hold his team together. This task requires the personnel officer's skills of man-management. He must be able to settle differences of opinion that emerge among his ministers, either by persuading dissenters to accept the majority view, or, if it becomes necessary, to dismiss, with the minimum of fuss, those who are undermining unity. Clashes between the Prime Minister and one of his ministers, leading to the latter's dismissal, are dramatic and newsworthy, and can be an indication that the Prime Minister possesses the required amount of determination and steel to be an effective leader. The much less spectacular settlement of disputes in private, by the gentle art of conciliation, is, however, of much more significance for the unity of the government in the long run. If the Prime Minister picks his team carefully in the first place, and conciliates effectively when conflicts do emerge, dramatic dismissals become unnecessary.

In order to exert control over the government's output (by which is meant executive actions, moral leadership, foreign policy initiatives, as well as legislation), the Prime Minister can adopt one of two approaches. On the one hand he can act as a "chairman of the board", using the skills of the arbitrator to coax a consensus from conflicting points of view in Cabinet, and persuade dissenters to accept the dominant view and live within collective responsibility. Alternatively, he can act as a more dynamic "managing director", using the skills of the innovator to devise his own solutions to problems, and then impose his initiatives upon his ministerial colleagues. For the "chairman of the board" approach the Prime Minister has to be somewhat self-effacing, subordinating his own view to the collective view. For the "managing director" approach he has to have the personal prestige, talent, and strength of will to enable him to dominate his colleagues. A Prime Minister will adopt each of these approaches at one time or another. Inevitably, however, he will incline more towards one than the other, depending on his own character and personality, his prestige with the public and with his ministers, the abilities and status of these ministers, and the variety of opinions that exist among them, which in turn will be dependent upon the way he has performed his earlier role of recruiting officer.

Finally, for the task of representing the government in negotiations with foreign governments, or with provincial governments or interest groups in Canada, the Prime Minister requires the skills of the ambassador. He has to be able to present the national point of view in the most favourable light, and defend the national interest in secret negotiations, while preserving cordial relations with the several parties concerned.

d. "Selling" the Government

A basic principle of democratic politics, as of law, is that not only must justice be done, it must be seen to be done. More than this, even when justice is *not* done political leaders must try to make it *appear* as if it is done. Governments ignore the art of public relations at their peril. As much as anything, the politician's task is to explain and persuade—to explain to the electorate what the government is doing, and to persuade them to accept it. In Canada the Prime Minister is the principal person to whom the public looks for this explanation and justification of government outputs. Inevitably, therefore, he becomes the government's chief public-relations officer. For this role he must be skilled in public pleading, capable of presenting a case in terms that will be understood by, and will capture the imagination of, his audience. The "audience", however, can be any one of the five "p's"—Parliament, party, pressure groups, press, and public. The form of the appeal that he will have to make, and the particular public relations skills he will require, will be different in each case. He will be able to adopt a blatantly partisan stance when facing party or pressure-group leaders in private, but when facing Parliament, the press, or the public he will have to talk more in terms of the broader national interest. Again, the particular style he will have to adopt for a television studio appearance will be different from that required when addressing a mass rally or a caucus meeting.

The Prime Minister's public-relations role is important in three distinct respects. First, in an open society political leaders have an obligation to explain what they are doing and why they are doing it. A flow of information between government and people is necessary if the public is to be able to identify with its rulers. There is clearly vast room for debate about precisely how much a government should reveal to the public. There is less room for argument, however, about the broad principle that, with the exception of matters that affect national security, the public has a right to be informed about government activities. As Benjamin Disraeli expressed the principle a century ago, "without publicity there can be no public spirit, and without public spirit every nation must decay."

Second, a wise Prime Minister will seek to smooth the way for his policies by persuading the public in general, and those most directly affected in particular, of the merits of those policies. Although some government policies are accepted only because the government uses its coercive power to enforce them, many others are accepted without coercion because the public recognizes, or is persuaded of, the desirability of the measure, and is prepared to co-operate in its implementation. A government that wishes to govern through a minimum of coercion and a maximum of consent has to devote a lot of attention to the task of achieving a high level of public sympathy for its general aims, and acceptance of its particular proposals.

Third, and most fundamental of all, a Prime Minister who wishes to retain office has to fight an election campaign, not just in the few weeks before polling day but throughout his period of office—which points to the final aspect of the prime-ministerial life-cycle.

e. Retaining the Post

The process of retaining his job brings the Prime Minister back to the beginning of the cycle—although to square two rather than to square one, in that he does not have to secure readoption as party leader. He must retain his party's confidence, of course, or the party may choose to replace him, and each party now has procedures for reviewing the leadership at regular intervals. The only serving Prime Minister to be overthrown by his party, however, was Mackenzie Bowell in 1896. Today the process of removing the leader is all the more difficult to achieve because both parties now use national Conventions to select their leaders, and there are practical difficulties in holding such a Convention when the party is in office.

The Prime Minister does have to fight a general election, however, at least every five years. Electoral studies have not thrown a great deal of light on the question of just how important the actual campaign is, as opposed to the government's longer term record, in determining the outcome of elections. It is clear, however, that a Prime Minister cannot afford to assume that a well-fought two-month campaign will remedy the neglect of public relations over the preceding four years. Prime Ministers have to guard their government's reputations throughout a Parliament.

The basic electoral strategy involved in seeking to retain power is essentially the same as that involved in attempting to gain office from Opposition. In each case it is necessary to capture the votes of non-committed electors while retaining the support of the party faithful. The task of defending a record, however, requires different tactics from that of attacking a record, and often the most profitable tactic is to divert public attention onto other matters, such as the personal qualities of the Prime Minister and the Leader of the Opposition.

THE MEN AND THE SKILLS

The prime-ministerial roles and skills referred to in the previous section are summarized in Table 2:5. To what extent have Canadian prime ministers possessed the required skills? Clearly, the ideal Prime Minister would possess them all to an equally well-developed degree. No one is likely to achieve such a degree of perfection, but in order to be regarded even as moderately successful, a Prime Minister cannot afford to be glaringly inadequate in any one of the roles. The measurement of "success" and "competence" in this context is, of course, very difficult, and because the judgment is highly subjective, examples inevitably are controversial. Nevertheless, by way of conclusions to this chapter, some tentative observations on the relative strengths and weaknesses of Canadian prime ministers are presented below and in Table 2:5.

Someone who cannot pose convincingly as a champion of party interests is unlikely to attain even the first base of becoming party leader. Even though Trudeau was relatively new to the Liberal Party in 1968, he had shown himself capable of defending Quebec Liberal interests. Walter Gordon, on the other hand, who might have aspired to the leadership of the Liberal Party, had difficulty in convincing large sections of the party that he was ideologically acceptable to them. If the party leader is unconvincing as a vote-catcher he will not be able to achieve office, unless the collective appeal exerted by the party is sufficiently strong to overcome his personal deficiencies. Mackenzie King was a master electioneer, and this gave him a vast hold over his party. Meighen, on the other hand, no matter how many other prime-ministerial qualities he possessed, lacked the fundamental skill of being able to win elections. Again, even though a party leader may persuade a majority of electors to support him, if, after the election, he fails to convince the other parties' supporters that he is a truly national leader, he will preside over a divided country. Diefenbaker inspired feelings of considerable affection and considerable distrust, and produced great tensions in Canadian society as a result. If, however, a Prime Minister goes too far in accommodating the interests of the other parties, he is liable to antagonize his own party supporters, as when Mackenzie King lost the support of many Ontario Liberals over the conscription issue in 1944.

If a Prime Minister cannot adapt the machinery of government so as to produce effective policy-making and decision-taking procedures, his government will become atrophied and

Table 2:5

PRIME-MINISTERIAL FUNCTIONS AND SKILLS

Function	Required Skill	Examples of PMs in Whom the Skill was	
		a) very well developed	b) less well developed
Acquiring the job			
Faction leader	Partisanship	Diefenbaker	
Election winner	Vote-catching	King	Meighen
National figurehead	Statesmanship	Laurier	Abbott
Forming a government			
Organization man	Structure building	Trudeau	St. Laurent
Recruiting officer	Staffing	Macdonald	Mackenzie
Leading a government			
Personnel officer	Man-management	St. Laurent	Bowell
Chairman of the board	Arbitration	Pearson	Bennett
Policy leadership ('managing director')	Innovation	Bennett	Pearson
Ambassador	Diplomacy	Borden	Diefenbaker
"Selling" the Government			
Publicity officer (Parl.)	Parl. pleading	Meighen	Trudeau
Publicity officer (public)	Public pleading	Diefenbaker	St. Laurent

inefficient. Trudeau and Pearson were both innovative in this respect, whereas St. Laurent largely made do with the structures developed by Mackenzie King. If a Prime Minister cannot persuade men of ability and influence to serve as ministers, he will produce a team that is untalented or unrepresentative, or both. Sir John A. Macdonald, in forming his first Cabinet, set the pattern of a regionally and ethnically representative team, and throughout his reign as Prime Minister he successfully balanced interests and talent in his Cabinet. In contrast, Conservative prime ministers in this century have all failed to make satisfactory Cabinet appointments from Quebec (even in 1958 when Diefenbaker had 50 Quebec MPs from which to choose).

Once the team is built, if the Prime Minister is unskilled in man-management he will not be able to hold it together. Mackenzie King was a master of the art of reconciling Cabinet conflict, or of isolating the dissenter if reconciliation was impossible. Bowell, on the other hand, was incapable of doing this, and faced a major Cabinet revolt as a result. If a Prime Minister cannot move his Cabinet, either by imposing his own wishes on his colleagues, or by producing a consensus through arbitration, the government's output will be poor, and confined to non-controversial issues. R. B. Bennett is perhaps the prime example of the "managing director" type of Prime Minister who pushed his Cabinet in directions he determined, while Lester Pearson was the "chairman of the board" who constantly sought a consensus on which to base decisions. John Diefenbaker, on the other hand, has been accused of carrying the search for consensus to the extreme, and of being prepared to take action only when there was virtual unanimity in Cabinet.[7] No matter how successful a Prime Minister may be in the domestic arena, if he lacks the skills of the international diplomat, and is out of his depth at head-of-state meetings, essential Canadian interests will suffer. Canadian Prime Ministers have always been involved in defending Canadian interests in dealings with her giant allies—Imperial Britain in the nineteenth century, and Imperial America in the twentieth. Borden and King both demonstrated great skill in this respect in wartime situations.

Finally, if he cannot advertise his government's policies adequately, they will meet resistance, no matter how worthy they may be in fact. Arthur Meighen was a particularly accomplished parliamentary performer, but he was much less effective outside the House, and was out-manoeuvred by Mackenzie King at the electoral level. Lester Pearson never mastered Parliamentary debating techniques, and disliked electioneering. John Diefenbaker, on the other hand, was in his element on the party platform and in the House, but was less convincing in Cabinet.

Thus the skills that the Prime Minister is required to possess are so numerous and so varied that it is almost inevitable that he will be found to be deficient in at least one of them. Thomas Jefferson's pessimistic judgment that "no man will ever bring out of the Presidency the reputation which carries him into it" applies equally well to the office of Prime Minister. Indeed there may be something of an "iron law" of unavoidable prime-ministerial failure: every Prime Minister will have an Achilles' heel on which critics can focus, so that no matter how successful he may be in most aspects of his job, his reputation is liable to be undermined by his lack of even one of the necessary talents. This, of course, can be true for Prime Ministers the world over. For the Prime Minister of Canada, however, things are made especially difficult by two particular aspects of Canadian political life. As suggested in Chapter One, there are features of Canadian politics which focus public attention on the Prime Minister and build up popular expectations of what he can personally achieve, while at the same time the practical restraints upon what a Canadian Prime Minister can achieve are vast. These two themes will be considered in some detail as subsequent chapters examine the various stages of the prime-ministerial life-cycle. In the next chapter the process by which a Prime Minister acquires the post will be examined, with particular emphasis on the factors that contribute to the personalization of Canadian politics.

NOTES

1. O. D. Skelton, *Life and Letters of Sir Wilfrid Laurier* (London: Oxford University Press, 1922) I:168.

2. "Canada and the Model of Westminster" in W. B. Hamilton, ed., *The Transfer of Institutions* (Durham N.C.: Duke University Press, 1964).

3. Peter C. Newman, *Renegade in Power* (Toronto: McClelland and Stewart, 1963), p. 12.

4. Thomas A. Hockin, *Apex of Power* (Scarborough: Prentice-Hall, 1971), p. 194.

5. Judy LaMarsh, *Memoirs of a Bird in a Gilded Cage* (Toronto: McClelland and Stewart, 1969), p. 62.

6. For details see below p. 143.

7. See, for example, Peter Stursburg, *Diefenbaker: Leadership Gained, 1956-62* (Toronto: University of Toronto Press, 1975), pp. 176-80.

3. The Greasy Pole

"I have climbed to the top of the greasy pole," said Benjamin Disraeli on first becoming British prime minister in 1868. In Canada, as in Britain, two basic unwritten constitutional rules govern who will have access to the pole. The first of these is that the aspiring Prime Minister must be a member of one of the houses of Parliament, or must become a member soon after appointment. Today convention demands that the Prime Minister be a member of the Commons rather than the Senate. In the 1890s Sir John Abbott and Sir Mackenzie Bowell held the post from the Senate, but all other Prime Ministers have been members of the Commons. The second basic rule is that the emerging Prime Minister must be the person best able to form a government that will command a majority in the Commons. In the context of modern parliamentary party politics this means that he must be the recognized leader of the party that has a majority of seats in the Commons, or, if no single party has an overall majority, the leader of the party that is best able to attract enough minor party support to give a government a working majority.

Within these two basic constitutional rules there are three distinct routes to the premiership. The first, and most direct, route involves the replacement of one Prime Minister by another from the same party while the party is in power. Seven appointments were made by this process: Sir John Abbott, 1891; Sir John Thompson, 1892; Sir Mackenzie Bowell, 1894; Sir Charles Tupper, 1896 (all during the Conservative Party's turmoils of the 1891-96 Parliament); Arthur Meighen, 1920; Louis St. Laurent, 1948; and Pierre Trudeau, 1968. In this situation it is theoretically possible for the new Prime Minister to be drawn from outside the Cabinet, or even outside Parliament, and parachuted into Parliament, the Cabinet, and the premiership at one and the same time. In practice, however, each of the seven direct entrants served in the Cabinet under his predecessor, so that in practical terms elevation to the premiership merely involved a move round the Cabinet table. The second and indirect route to the premiership is via the post of Leader of the Opposition. Mackenzie, 1873; Laurier, 1896; Borden, 1911; King, 1921; Bennett, 1930; Diefenbaker, 1957; and Pearson, 1963 followed this route. For these seven, elevation to the premiership involved a move across the floor of the House, rather than merely a move round the Cabinet table. Mackenzie made this move when Macdonald's government resigned after a parliamentary setback over the Pacific Scandal, and the others when the government resigned after losing its parliamentary majority at a general election. It took Laurier three general elections as Leader of the Opposition, and Pearson and Borden two, to reach power, but King, Bennett, and Diefenbaker achieved success in their first contests as Leader of the Opposition.

The third route is a variation of the second, and involves a former Prime Minister regaining the post after a spell in Opposition. This is a difficult task, and former Prime Ministers, like vanquished heavyweight boxing champions, rarely "come back". Only Macdonald, King, and Meighen have managed it. Macdonald in 1878, and King in 1926 and again in 1935, regained office within five years of losing it, after an electoral triumph, but Meighen's return to power was in the unusual circumstances of the 1926 constitutional crisis, and only lasted three months. Tupper, Laurier, and Diefenbaker attempted to regain office, but suffered further electoral defeats. Laurier subsequently died while Leader of the Opposition, Tupper retired soon after losing the 1900 election, and Diefenbaker was removed from the party leadership. Mackenzie, Bennett, St. Laurent, and Meighen (after his second spell as Prime Minister) retired from the party leadership during the Parliament following their loss of office.

THE FORMAL PROCESS

Whichever route is followed, the formal appointment of a

Prime Minister is made by the Governor General, acting on authority vested in him by the monarch. How smoothly does the selection process work, and how much room is there for a Governor General to exercise real discretion in the choice of Prime Minister? The process by which Sir John A. Macdonald became Canada's first Prime Minister in 1867 was wholly exceptional, as the first Parliament of the new Confederation had not been elected at the time of his appointment.[1] The Governor General, Lord Monck, had designated Macdonald for the task of leading the new nation following his performance as chairman of the 1866-67 Confederation Conference in London. In May 1867 Macdonald was formally invited to form a government to take office on July 1, 1867, and he duly accepted. Apart from this once-and-for-all situation, the Governor General has rarely had to exercise any real initiative in the selection of a Prime Minister.

In the first place, it has invariably been clear which party has been in the best position to form a government. Twenty-three of the twenty-nine general elections since Confederation have produced clear overall majorities for one or other of the two main parties. The other six elections (five of them in the period since 1957) produced a House of Commons in which no party had an overall majority, but for the most part these "indecisive" elections did not lead to problems over the succession. At the 1962 and 1972 elections the established government lost its overall majority but remained the largest single party, and stayed in office with the tolerance of the minor parties. In 1965 the minority Liberal government failed to win the overall majority that it had sought, but it remained the largest party and retained office. In 1957 and 1963 the Opposition party won more seats than the government but was short of an overall majority. On both occasions the government resigned before meeting Parliament, and the Leader of the Opposition was summoned to form a minority government. At the 1925 election the Liberal government won fewer seats than the Conservatives, but the Liberals remained in office with the support of the Progressives. Only after some months did a major constitutional crisis develop out of this situation. Thus Governors-General have not been called upon to exercise discretion over the question of which *party* should form the government. What is more, Governors-General have rarely had any difficulty in deciding which *member* of the dominant party was best placed to lead a government drawn from that party. On six of the seven occasions when the premiership has fallen vacant during a Parliament, the ruling party, by one means or another, clearly indicated its choice of leader, and the Governor General accepted this choice. The one exception was in 1894, when difficulties arose through John Thompson's sudden death, and the aversion of the Governor General, Lord Aberdeen, to the most obvious successor, Sir Charles Tupper.[2] Lord Aberdeen took soundings in Ottawa and London, but then, on his own initiative, sent for Mackenzie Bowell, even though Bowell's claim to the succession (and his talents) were generally regarded as limited.

Equally, on all but one of the occasions when a government has resigned following a general election defeat or a setback in the Commons, the acknowledged Leader of the Opposition has succeeded to the premiership without a hitch. The one exception was in 1873, when some doubts arose because although Alexander Mackenzie had been elected leader by the Liberal MPs the previous year, Edward Blake was widely regarded as the most talented and dynamic Liberal MP, who might head a Liberal government even though he had declined to lead the party in Opposition.[3] In the event, the Governor General sent for Mackenzie without delay, and he accepted the premiership.

Thus the prime-ministerial successions in Canada have always been smooth. Only in the 1925-26 Parliament was there any difficulty in deciding which party should form the government, and only in 1894, and to a lesser extent in 1873, was the Governor General called upon to exercise any real initiative in determining which member of the dominant party had the best claim to lead it. Because today all the parties have precise and public methods of selecting a leader, the room for real initiative by the Governor General is reduced even further. Problems could arise, of course, in a crisis situation, caused, perhaps, by the sudden death of the Prime Minister, or by a Cabinet revolt. In such a situation a temporary Prime Minister might have to be found to serve until the Government party could organize a national Convention to select a new leader. In such a crisis the Governor General might be involved in the selection process in more than a formal capacity.

The choice of Prime Minister could also be complicated if an increase in NDP support produced three fairly evenly balanced parties in the Commons, all claiming the right to form a government. Equally, selection problems could arise if developments in the party system produced a change from single-party governments to coalition governments. In Canada's only coalition governments, formed in 1867 and 1917, the leader of the dominant party was Prime Minister, but in a coalition the Prime Minister often has to be someone other than one of the party leaders. Above all, a coalition Prime Minister has to be acceptable to all the partners in the coalition, and as is sometimes the case in, for example, Italy and the Netherlands, a relatively innocuous minor figure has to be selected because the parties cannot agree to accept any of their established leaders. Even in these hypothetical situations, however, the Governor General would be only one of the figures involved in the negotiations to produce a Prime Minister, and his role might still be no more than the largely formal one of approving the agreed choice of the party leaders.

BECOMING PARTY LEADER

Apart from Arthur Meighen, all Prime Ministers since 1918 were selected to become party leaders at leadership Conventions. St. Laurent in 1948 and Trudeau in 1968 were selected at Conventions held while the party was in office, and subsequently became Prime Minister within weeks of the Convention. King, Bennett, Diefenbaker, and Pearson were selected at Conventions held while the party was in Opposition, and then became Prime Minister when a general election brought their party to power. What are the main features, and the main implications for the Canadian political system, of the Convention method of selecting party leaders?

a. The Politics of Leadership Conventions

The principal features of the Canadian Convention system can be briefly stated.[4] Leadership Conventions are not held on a regular basis, but only when a vacancy arises. Thus the Conservatives have held seven in fifty years (1927, 1938, 1942, 1948, 1956, 1967, and 1976), and the Liberals only four (1919, 1948, 1958, and 1968), with Mackenzie King's particularly long reign producing a gap of almost thirty years between the party's first and second Conventions. In a situation where the Prime Minister dies, or is suddenly overthrown, a caretaker Prime Minister would have to be appointed until the Convention machinery could be brought into operation. Of the fifteen Prime Ministers, Macdonald and Thompson died in office, and Bowell was overthrown, but all three in the 1890s before the Convention system was in use. In 1963, however, when Diefenbaker was almost deposed, the rebels had tentative arrangements to make George Nowlan caretaker Prime Minister while a Convention sought a successor.[5]

When a Convention does take place it is not necessarily linked with a general election, although if the party is in office it may seek a dissolution soon after the Convention in order to capitalize on the publicity received by the party and its new leader — as the Liberals did in 1948 and 1968. Recent Conventions have been large gatherings, with more than 2,400 attending the 1968 Liberal Convention, and 2,500 the 1976 Conservative Convention. The bulk of the delegates are chosen at the constituency level, so that the Conventions are not dominated by national or provincial-party hierarchies. What is more, voting is secret and by individuals, rather than open and by state delegations as it is at American presidential Conventions. The 1968 and 1976 Conventions lasted for three days, with the first two days nominally devoted to the consideration of party policy. In fact, policy discussion is completely subordinated to the process of selecting the leader.

Clearly, Conventions are potentially divisive. During 1967, for example, a "liberal" faction within Pearson's Cabinet met on a regular basis in order to devise a strategy to prevent the party's "conservatives" from capturing the leadership on Pearson's retirement.[6] Again, the open public campaigning prior to the Convention, and then the stylized confrontation at the Convention itself, might be expected to highlight regional, ethnic, or ideological divisions within the party more dramatically than would the brief and secret process of selection by caucus. In practice this danger is reduced by the party's awareness of the electoral implications of its deliberations, and by the potential leader's desire to inherit a united party and thus to keep the loyalty of the defeated candidates and their supporters. Further, when, as in 1968 and 1976, there are a large number of candidates, and thus a series of ballots, a candidate has to avoid offending his opponents' supporters in case he has to attract their votes in the later ballots. Thus the appeal of serious candidates tends to be non-abrasive and non-ideological, designed to appeal to as many shades of opinion as possible. Personality takes precedence over policy.

In 1919 Mackenzie King captured the Convention with a speech that simply attacked the Unionist government and eulogized Laurier.[7] At the 1958 Liberal Convention, neither Paul Martin nor Lester Pearson took firm policy stands, and Norman Ward remarked:

> In a literal sense, one of the distinguishing characteristics of the [1958] Convention was that it was itself clearly leaderless. . . . The battle for leadership, virtually stripped of references to "I will, if elected . . ." perforce became largely a popularity contest. . . .[8]

Much the same comment could have been made about the 1968 Liberal Convention. Television coverage of the pre-Convention campaign helped Trudeau to base his appeal on personality, and at the Convention his performance was platitudinous in the extreme. Insofar as his aim was to win the leadership while maintaining party unity, he would seem to have succeeded. Even though Trudeau secured just 51 per cent of the votes in the final ballot, survey evidence suggests that 96 per cent of the delegates were satisfied with the outcome, and 86 per cent thought the selection of Trudeau had improved the party's electoral prospects.[9] Thus the traditional display of party unity at the end of the Convention, with defeated candidates proposing and seconding the unanimous adoption of the winner, is not without significance.

In the process of attracting delegate support a candidate will endeavour to create as few obligations as possible, so as to leave himself with maximum freedom of movement if he does become party leader. The absence of serious policy discussions at Conventions means that, for the most part, candidates can avoid making policy commitments, while the system of voting by secret ballot means that votes cannot be "delivered" by individuals, groups, or regions, in return for favours. In these respects Canadian Conventions differ markedly from American presidential Conventions, which operate on the principle of open support being given in return for policy commitments or other favours. Inevitably, however, a candidate at a Canadian Convention will become obligated to those who gave him financial backing, and as campaign costs can be very high, all but the wealthiest candidates will incur some such debts. A candidate will also have obligations to those who campaigned for him, or who endorsed his candidature. Trudeau's success in 1968, for example, owed much to long-standing support by Jean Marchand, and last minute endorsement by Mitchell Sharp — and both were rewarded with senior posts when Trudeau formed his Cabinet. In the interests of party unity, the new leader will also be obliged to compensate those he defeated in the leadership contest. Indeed, some candidates enter the leadership race merely to improve their chances of promotion after the contest. John Turner's decision at the 1968 Convention to remain in the contest to the final ballot, even though he trailed well behind the leading contestants, was almost certainly based on such a consideration.

Leadership selection by a Convention rather than by caucus increases the chances of a candidate being chosen who has only limited parliamentary experience. King at the first Liberal Convention in 1919, and Bennett at the first Conservative Convention in 1927, were selected in preference to more experienced parliamentary figures, and this pattern has often been repeated. Indeed, it seems to be almost a principle of the Canadian Convention system that "the less the Parliamentary experience, the greater the chances of success". The Liberals have tended to look for administrative experience gained in the public service, rather than for strictly parliamentary experience, while the Conservatives have looked to provincial politics for many of their leadership candidates, perhaps because over the last fifty years it is only at the provincial level that Conservatives have been able to gain much executive experience. The selection of a leader with limited or no parliamentary experience could complicate his relationship with caucus. The majority of caucus may well have preferred someone else. In 1967, for example, Robert Stanfield was faced by a largely pro-Diefenbaker caucus, and this delayed his acceptance at the parliamentary level. Even if caucus approves of the new leader, however, the fact remains that it did not select him: he does not owe his position to caucus even though the essence of the Canadian parliamentary-Cabinet system is government responsibility to Parliament.

b. The Benefits of Conventions

It is clear, then, that the Convention method of selecting party leaders has many limitations. It is a long, drawn-out, and expensive process, and a serious candidate has to be wealthy or have wealthy backers. It is liable to produce leaders lacking parliamentary and ministerial skills, and it complicates the relationship between the leader and his parliamentary colleagues. On the whole, it is a system that is more suitable for presidential than for parliamentary constitutions. While acknowledging these factors, does the system confer any benefits on the party as a whole, and on the party leader in particular?

Having been selected at a Convention the leader enjoys a considerable degree of security of tenure: a Cabinet or caucus revolt is not enough to unseat him. Conventions are not held on any regular basis, and unless the leader has died or has agreed to retire, they are not easily summoned. Although each party now has a process for reviewing the leadership, the opportunities for review are limited, and even if a Convention does result from these procedures, the established leader might well be re-elected. The leader's position in Parliament can be enhanced by the fact that he became party leader at a Convention made up of delegates from all sections of the party. In caucus and in Cabinet he can speak with the authority of someone selected by a truly *national* gathering. The caucus may not be representative of all the provinces. In 1919, for example, three-quarters of the Liberal MPs were from Quebec, and this was a major reason for using a Convention, rather than a caucus ballot, to select Laurier's successor.[10] In recent years the Liberals have rarely had many MPs from the west, while throughout this century the Conservatives have invariably been weak in Quebec. Equally, while the Cabinet as a whole might be nationally representative, each particular member is seen to be a representative of a particular region. Thus in confrontations with Cabinet or caucus the leader can point to the grass-roots basis of his authority, and can argue that he represents the party and the nation as a whole, while his colleagues merely represent constituencies or regions.

Important electoral consequences of the system should also be noted. A leadership Convention can improve a party's electoral prospects, in that Convention publicity helps to advertise the party and its new leader. The 1927 Conservative Convention received coast-to-coast coverage by radio, and the 1956 Conservative Convention was the first in Canada to be covered by television. The 1967, 1968, and 1976 Conventions, and the campaigns that preceded them, attracted vast television coverage, and presumably the pattern has now been set for the future. Media coverage inevitably concentrates on the candidates, and thus adds to the personalization of Canadian politics. It also serves to overcome the lack of interest in, and awareness of, national politics in federal, regionalized Canada, and to this extent it is an integrative force in Canadian politics. What is more, because Conventions are not held at fixed intervals, they can be timed so as to obtain publicity for the party as an election approaches. The Opposition party can call a Convention when it thinks that an election is due, but the real initiative is with the government party, which controls the timing of the election as well as of its own Convention. To make full use of its advantages, of course, the government party would have to change its leader once per Parliament, and such a strategy is hardly practical. In 1948 and 1968, however, the Liberals did successfully pursue the strategy of holding a Convention to select a new leader, and then calling a general election to capitalize on the publicity from the Convention.

A Convention is a sound means of finding a leader who has

electoral appeal. The delegates at a Convention represent a broad cross-section of the nation. What is more, in contrast to the more intimate processes of Cabinet or caucus selection, the Convention delegates have relatively little knowledge of the candidates. Robert Stanfield, for example, was little known by Conservatives outside Nova Scotia before 1967, while Trudeau had made little national impact before 1968. Thus the appeal that a relatively unknown candidate has to make in order to win delegate support at the Convention is similar to the appeal he will later have to make to attract electoral support. Laurier was aware of this in advocating the use of a Convention to select his successor:

> A leader who could win the delegates might conceivably win an election. . . . The delegates were to help in the discovery of the right man and the right formula for electoral success.[11]

The significance of this assumption, however, will be examined in more detail in the next two sections.

THE PRIME MINISTER AND GENERAL ELECTIONS

a. Prime-Ministerial Campaigning

What role is played by the Prime Minister and the other party leaders in general election campaigns? In the post-war period, John Diefenbaker and Pierre Trudeau have been associated particularly with "presidential" style campaigns, but they were certainly not the first Canadian party leaders to emphasize personal rather than party appeal. In 1891 the Conservative campaign slogan was "The old flag, the old man, and the old policy", with Conservative candidates fighting behind this cry. The election campaigns of the 1920s and 1930s were to a considerable extent personal duels between Meighen and King, and then Bennett and King. Bennett ran his elections, like his government, on one-man lines. The Liberal slogans in 1935 were "King or Chaos" and "Bennett let us down: drive him out", thereby emphasizing personalities rather than policies. In 1949, with each party having a newly selected leader, the contest became a personal choice between St. Laurent and Drew. In 1953 the Liberal campaign again concentrated on presenting "Uncle Louis" rather than policy issues, and the Liberal slogan was "A Great Leader for a Greater Canada". J. M. Beck comments that:

> What interest there was [in the 1953 election] centred on the leaders and their meetings. The use of modern advertising techniques in electioneering made this inevitable. Ad-men, not wishing to spread their sales pitch too thin, concentrated on the big names.[12]

The five campaigns that the Conservative Party fought under Diefenbaker's leadership were all highly personalized appeals. The 1957 election came only six months after the Convention at which Diefenbaker became leader. The Conservative campaign was given a big boost by the Convention, and in effect Diefenbaker campaigned continuously throughout the period from the Convention to the election. The main Conservative slogan in 1957 was "It's time for a Diefenbaker Government". Peter C. Newman has described vividly the opening meeting of the campaign, in Toronto's Massey Hall, which set the tone for the whole campaign:

> Elephantine enlargements of Diefenbaker photographs smiled down at the audience of 2,600 enthusiastic supporters, while on stage fifty of the Party's Ontario candidates sat before a thirty-foot-high map of Canada, bearing the legend "Diefenbaker—Canada's Man". The word "Conservative" was nowhere in evidence.[13]

The 1958 campaign was even more personalized than that of 1957, with Conservative candidates claiming to be "Diefenbaker's representatives". In 1962, after five years in office, Diefenbaker was presented as the personification of the Government of Canada, with the Conservative appeal being to "re-elect the Prime Minister". In the main Conservative pamphlet for this election Diefenbaker was mentioned eleven times, but the name of his party only once.[14]

Faced with these highly personalized appeals by the Conservatives, the Liberals attempted to reply in kind, at least in 1957 and 1958. John Meisel has said of the 1957 Liberal campaign:

> Mr. St. Laurent—considered the most valuable asset of the

party—was linked to the generally good conditions in the country. Uncle Louis—this time . . . ever more frequently and openly emphasising the family image—was identified with Canada's development and prosperity. And Uncle Louis was, of course, linked inseparably to the Liberal party.[15]

In 1958 Lester Pearson also tried to match Diefenbaker's personal appeal, but with little success. In the 1962, 1963, and 1965 campaigns, therefore, the Liberals sought to present a more collective image to the electorate. Thus in 1962 the main Liberal slogan was "Take a stand for tomorrow" as opposed to the Conservatives "Diefenbaker, the man for all Canada". In 1965, as Prime Minister, Pearson campaigned very little, remaining in Ottawa for much of the time, and relying on a general image of executive competence to attract votes to the party.

With the election of Trudeau as leader, the Liberals reverted to personalized campaigning. The 1968 election came just two months after the Liberal leadership Convention, and nine months after the Conservative Convention, and was fought very much on the basis of a choice between two new party leaders (and two contrasting types of party leader). Peter Regenstreif concluded that "the election is a plebiscite on leadership" while J. M. Beck's verdict was that:

> More than ever before, the [1968] election had been presidential rather than parliamentary—a contest between Trudeau and Stanfield—and candidates of quality had counted for nought.[16]

In 1972 also, the emphasis was on a personal appeal, with Trudeau largely ignoring policy and merely asking the voters to re-elect him for a further term. In 1974 the Opposition parties tried to focus attention on the particular issues of the cost of living and inflation. The Liberals, however, again sought, with considerable success, to capitalize on Trudeau's leadership qualities, mantaining that "inflation is the problem, leadership the issue".

Thus at least one of the two main parties has usually made its leader the centre of its electoral appeal. It should not be concluded, however, that Canadian general elections are necessarily "presidential" in character, and clear distinctions should be made between "presidential", "semi-presidential", and "non-presidential" contests. Some elections clearly *are* presidential in that *both* main parties focus their campaign on the appeal of their leader. The 1957 St. Laurent-*versus*-Diefenbaker, and the 1968 Trudeau-*versus*-Stanfield contests were presidential, with electors being asked to choose between two men rather than two parties or two sets of policies. Many other elections, however, are merely semi-presidential, in that one party focuses on its leader while the other bases its appeal on policy or on the party's collective face. In 1963 and 1965 the Conservatives focused on Diefenbaker and the Liberals on a more collective appeal, while in 1974 the Conservatives concentrated on the specific issue of inflation and the Liberals emphasized "leadership". Equally, some contests are non-presidential or parliamentary, in that both parties present a collective face, or concentrate on issues rather than personalities. The 1917 election, for example, was very much an "issue election" fought over the conscription question, while in 1887 the Riel affair, and in 1896 the Manitoba schools issue, dominated the campaign. In such elections the over-riding importance of one issue leaves no room for the more ephemeral appeal of personalities.

b. The Electoral Reaction

To what extent are electoral loyalties in Canada based on the attraction of the party leaders? Political science research into voting behaviour has now produced a lot of information on the way people vote (the extent to which ethnic, religious, social, and other groupings within society support particular parties), but there is much less information on why people vote the way they do (the factors that attract a voter or group of voters to a particular party). Studies of voting behaviour in recent Canadian elections, however, have provided some evidence of the importance of the appeal exerted by the party leaders. During the 1962 and 1963 campaigns Peter Regenstreif asked a national sample of electors why they intended to support a particular party.[17] With the Liberal and minor party voters "party identification" was the principal motivating factor, but with Conservative voters "leader appeal" rivalled party identification (see Table 3:1). Regenstreif also asked his sample who they would like to see as Prime Minister, regardless of their own party preference. Of Conservative voters, three-quarters in 1962 and two-thirds in 1963, plumped for Diefenbaker, but among Liberal voters the numbers who preferred leaders other than Pearson, together with the number of "don't knows", indicated a clear conflict between party loyalty and lack of enthusiasm for their leader. Regenstreif concluded that:

> The personal style of the Diefenbaker candidacy and the party-oriented nature of Pearson's support holds true for the three elections in which these leaders were opponents and is reflected in the remarks made by respondents in those campaigns.[18]

John Meisel has produced some evidence of the factors that attracted voters to the parties in the 1968 election.[19] In a post-election survey a national sample was asked whether the leader, the local candidate, the party as a whole, or the MP's record was the most important in influencing the way they voted (see Table 3:2). More than half of the Liberal voters opted for the leader, and a third for the party. With the other parties' voters, however, party appeal was of more importance, with only a

TABLE 3:1

FACTORS IN PARTY PREFERENCE—1962 AND 1963 ELECTIONS

Response to question: "What is the most important reason you have for saying [you will support a particular party]?"

	1962				1963			
	Lib	PC	NDP	SC	Lib	PC	NDP	SC
Party identification	47	35	31	29	38	29	43	16
Leader	3	32	12	10	6	30	3	7
Domestic issues	25	6	24	24	5	2	24	15
Other or no reason	51	51	67	59	77	59	70	80

Columns do not add up to 100 per cent as some respondents quoted more than one reason.

SOURCE: Adapted from data in Peter Regenstreif, *The Diefenbaker Interlude* (Don Mills: Longmans, 1965), p. 74.

TABLE 3:2

FACTORS IN PARTY PREFERENCE—1968 ELECTION

Response to question: "In deciding what you would do in this recent election, which was most important to you: the leaders, the work of the MPs, your local candidate, or the parties taken as a whole?"

	Lib	PC	NDP	RC/SC
Leader	51	32	24	24
MP's work	7	8	11	22
Local candidate	9	25	20	22
Party	32	35	46	33

SOURCE: John Meisel, *Working Papers On Canadian Politics* (Montreal: McGill University Press, 1972), p. 31.

third or a quarter quoting leader appeal: for NDP voters in particular, "personality" (whether of the leader or the local candidate) mattered less than the "ideological" appeal of the party as a whole. Thus Meisel observed:

> We see that the Liberals alone rated the leader in first place—a development which must be ascribed to Mr. Trudeau's extraordinary appeal to an important segment of the 1968 Canadian electorate.[20]

Following the 1974 election, a nation-wide survey by J. Pammett *et al.* suggested that Trudeau's appeal was a less important factor in attracting voters to the Liberals than it had been in 1968.[21] Nevertheless, the survey indicated that among the factors determining electoral choice in 1974, Liberal voters, unlike Conservative and NDP voters, still rated the appeal of the leader higher than that of the local candidate or the party as a whole.

There are indications that the appeal of the party leaders is a particularly important factor among new voters, uncommitted voters, and floating voters, who, of course, make up the vital groups in determining election results. Pammett *et al.*, for example, found that in 1974 the party leader's appeal counted for even more among those who were voting for the first time than it did among older voters.[22] In a survey conducted in three Hamilton constituencies during the 1968 campaign, Winham and Cunningham found that Trudeau's appeal was instrumental in developing interest in the election, and in encouraging the normally non-involved electors to vote.[23] They also found that among usually uncommitted electors, and also among those who in 1968 voted differently from 1965, favourable perceptions of the party leader were a major factor in determining voting behaviour. Winham and Cunningham concluded:

> Voting theories have tended to stress the fixed factors in the electorate—regionalism, ethnic origin, religion, or class—in an effort to establish patterns of voting participation. However, these patterns apply mainly to those voters who identify themselves with a major party. This omits from the calculus the group of uncommitted voters plus party switchers, a group whose behaviour is less likely to be affected by fixed social factors and more likely to be affected by idiosyncratic factors which develop in different campaigns, such as the personality of the national party leaders.[24]

The appeal of the party leader, then, can be seen as being of particular importance in the existing multi-party situation in Canada. Five of the eight elections over the last twenty years have been "indecisive" in the sense that no party won an overall majority. One interpretation of these results is that indecisive elections have become the Canadian "norm", other than when a sufficiently charismatic leader, through his personal appeal, can attract sufficient "extra" votes to his party to give it an overall majority.

The importance of the leader's electoral appeal is a product of various aspects of Canadian society and politics — perhaps the most important being the relatively low level of image-difference between the two parties. It is a widely held view among students of electoral attitudes in Canada that the voter perceives very little difference between the two parties in terms of their policies or general image, and that electoral loyalties are relatively easily broken.[25] Howard S. Scarrow, for example, argues that while there are broad differences in image between the two main Canadian parties, these are less than those between the two American parties, with economic and policy considerations playing little part in determining electoral choice.[26] Robert Alford has made a similar point, arguing that:

> The political parties in Canada may approximate more closely than those in other countries to the classic description of parties as men temporarily associated because of the necessities of the strategy of power.[27]

Electoral studies have shown that while Canadians may readily identify with a particular party, their allegiance to the party is comparatively loosely held. Recent surveys indicate, for example, that compared with British and American electors a large proportion of Canadians are prepared to vote for one party while continuing to identify with another.[28] Thus a post-election survey in 1965 found that compared with 1963, 15 per cent of electors reported a change of vote without any accompanying change of party identification.

Perhaps as a result of spending almost twenty consecutive years in office in the crisis periods before, during, and after the Second World War, the Liberal Party has acquired an image of managerial competence which can be appealing to all the electors equally. The Conservative Party, in more recent years, has sought to match this type of appeal. In such calculatedly non-ideological and non-group-oriented appeals, there is considerable scope for personality considerations to emerge as vital factors determining the level of electoral support. Further, the national organization of the parties is fairly weak, and is geared to leader control. The influence of American presidential politics is strong. As stressed earlier, the Convention system (itself, to some extent, a reflection of American influences) focuses public attention on the parties through personalities rather than through policies. In particular, in an election that follows soon after a leadership Convention, as, for example, the elections of 1949, 1957, and 1968, the public awareness of the new leader (or, as in 1949 and 1968, the *two* new leaders) will be sustained into the election campaign.

The influence of the modern mass media is very important in this context. As J. R. Mallory has observed, soon after Diefenbaker's spectacular 1958 victory, ". . . money and organization are not enough unless a party can project an image of itself which gets a strong response from the voters. The intervention of television has undoubtedly brought much closer together the visible personality of the Prime Minister or party leader, and the image which the party wishes to project of itself to the voters."[29]

This is not to suggest, of course, that the personalization of Canadian elections dates only from the radio and television age. Even in the nineteenth century the leader's role was often crucial in determining the election result. Sir John A. Macdonald's personal drawing power was undoubted. He claimed personal credit for the Conservative victory in 1872, arguing that but for his own personal efforts "I do not think that a corporal's guard of Ministerialists would have been returned."[30] Similarly, in the 1896 campaign the two party leaders, Tupper and Laurier, dominated the fight, and Laurier was widely credited with the Liberal success.[31] As noted in the previous section, however, over the last twenty years or so the impact of radio and television has revolutionized election campaigning. The general effect has been to emphasize even further the personality orientation of the Canadian parties.

Again, compared with many countries, Canadian society contains a high proportion of immigrants, migrants, and young voters. These social groups often lack firm political roots and have been shown by comparative voting-behaviour research to respond to personality rather than policy factors. To some extent, of course, the importance of the appeal of the party leaders in determining electoral preferences is merely a consequence of the fact that in their election campaigns the parties focus a lot of attention on the leader. This argument, however, is clearly circular: the elector's choice is determined to a considerable extent by the leaders' personalities; therefore, the parties focus a lot of attention on their leaders; therefore, the elector's choice is bound to be determined to a considerable extent by the leaders' personalities.

NATIONAL LEADERSHIP

Having captured the party leadership, and then led his party to electoral success, how readily can the new Prime Minister gain acceptance as a national leader rather than merely a faction leader? Inevitably, the ease with which the transition can be made will depend to some extent upon the manner in which the election campaign was conducted. If the contest was fought on extremely partisan lines, with divisive issues being highlighted, and bitter attacks made on other parties, post-election reconciliation is difficult. Equally, if great attention was focused on the leader during the election, he will be more easily converted into a national symbol than if he was buried within an all-embracing collective or ideological appeal. The bigger the victory, and the more evenly the winning party's seats are spread throughout the country, the easier will be the task of gaining national acceptance. Thus Diefenbaker in 1958 could truly claim to be the "national" choice, having secured a majority of the votes and seats in every province except Newfoundland. After some other elections, however, notably the "conscription" and "manpower" elections of 1917 and 1945 (when the Liberals were particularly dominant in Quebec and the Conservatives in Ontario), truly national acceptance of the government and its leader is more difficult to achieve.

A Canadian prime minister's role as national leader is complicated by the fact that he is not head of state. Dawson and Ward, for example, argue that:

> Pomp, ceremony, and the external symbols of power and high regard are lavished on the one executive, while the other (though supported of course by a majority in the House of Commons) must in contrast rest content with an occasional expression of popular confidence moderated at all times by systematic opposition and carping criticism.[32]

Compared with constitutional relationships in the U.S.A. and Fifth Republic France, this is a fair comment. The strength of American and French presidents is based partly on the absence of any other national figurehead to detract from their prestige. This practice is, in effect, an expression of the medieval principle of the omnipotent monarch who combines symbolic and political roles. It is unusual in the modern western world, however, and most countries are like Canada in having a purely symbolic head of state, be it a figurehead monarch as in Sweden, Britain, and the Netherlands, or a figurehead president as in Italy, Ireland, and West Germany.

In Canada, of course, the distinction between head of state and head of government is further complicated in that the Queen delegates many of her functions as head of state to her "agent", the Governor General. Thus there are in Canada three national symbols — the Queen as head of state, the Governor General as the Canadian-based "deputy head of state", and the Prime Minister as the head of government. Because of this, the Canadian Prime Minister is perhaps not as disadvantaged as Dawson and Ward maintain. The monarch is foreign-born and resident abroad. For much of the Canadian population the preservation of the historic British connection through the monarch is at best an irrelevance, and at worst a source of constant friction. Even the most successful of royal tours will have only a limited impact upon the third of the population who are of French-Canadian descent, or the quarter who are of neither British nor French ethnic stock.

Since 1947 the Governor General has exercised almost all the prerogative power of the Crown, and since 1952 the holders of the office have all been Canadian born and bred. The Governor General, however, lacks the mystique of an actual monarch. He is an appointed figure, rather than an elected or hereditary one, and as a rule he holds office for only one five-year term. The Canadian-born Governors-General have not been altogether free from "political" backgrounds. Massey was a minister under King and a President of the National Liberal Federation; Vanier was an ambassador and public servant; Mitchener was a Conservative MP before becoming Speaker of the Commons. Despite attempts to increase the Governor General's prestige by seeking international recognition for his role as *de facto* head of state (in 1971, for example, he, rather than the Queen, was Canada's representative at the ceremonies to mark 2,500 years of the Persian Empire), he remains essentially the delivery boy rather than the grocer, and his subordinate status is high-lighted whenever the monarch does make a personal appearance in Canada.

A survey conducted by John Meisel in 1968 indicated that there was no great enthusiasm for the monarchy, taking the nation as a whole, but that it was a divisive issue in so far as French- and English-speaking Canadians had markedly differing attitudes: 60 per cent of French-Canadians felt that the monarchy should be abolished, compared with just 30 per cent of English-Canadians, with those of other ethnic stock being closer to French-Canadian than to English-Canadian attitudes.[33] Meisel's sample was also asked to assess the relative importance of certain public offices, including the Prime Minister, the Governor General, and the Queen. Roughly two-thirds of the respondents cited the federal Prime Minister as being "important", compared with only a quarter who saw the Queen or Governor General as important. The Prime Minister was at the top of the rankings, with the Queen twelfth, and the Governor General thirteenth, ranked lower than judges, the local mayor, the armed forces, and federal and provincial ministers and MPs.

Thus there would seem to be some justification for Peter C. Newman's claim that:

> Lacking a resident monarchy, Canadians have elevated their Prime Minister to a position of prestige as high as that found in any parliamentary democracy.[34]

The position into which he has been elevated is somewhat lower than that of the head of government in the U.S.A. or France, who has no competition from a separate head of state, but is probably higher than that of the head of government in countries like Britain or Sweden, where the figurehead is not dual-headed as it is in Canada.

CONCLUSIONS

The Convention method of selecting a party leader, the vital role that the leader plays in determining the outcome of a general election, and his post-election status as a national figurehead, all serve to focus public attention on the Prime Minister. Four particular consequences of this should be noted. First, emphasis on personality provides a degree of flexibility for the party system. It makes possible radical new developments, in that the emergence of a new leader can change completely a party's image, and its electoral prospects. In 1957, for example, the electoral appeal that the Conservative Party was able to make, based on Diefenbaker's personal image rather than upon policy or general party image, served to cloak the fact that the party had spent almost two decades in Opposition, that none of its potential ministers had any federal executive experience, and that it had few credible policies. Similarly, the extent to which Trudeau captured the public imagination in 1968 enabled the Liberals to make something of a fresh start, despite having spent five indifferent years in office. As J. M. Beck has commented about the Liberal appeal, and the electoral reaction to it, in 1968:

> [the voters] divorced a Trudeau Government consisting almost entirely of hold-overs from anything that preceded it. Some Liberals even asked to be elected to help Trudeau get the country moving again, forgetting that a Liberal Government had held office for five years.[35]

Second, leader appeal can have a unifying effect upon the Canadian electorate. Response to the appeal of the national leader, rather than to the more parochial appeal of the local candidate, has a centralizing effect on attitudes. Again, because voting patterns based on the appeal of party leaders are fairly transitory, they will be less divisive than voting patterns that correspond to the more fundamental and long standing cleavages within society, like religion, class, or ethnicity. The rigidity of say, Italian or Irish party loyalties is avoided. The result, of course, is a degree of electoral instability, and a brand of "pop-star" politics in which public attention is diverted from "real" issues by the comparatively trivial considerations of personal style and appearance. Nevertheless, basic social divisions are undermined rather than reinforced, and this is of some importance for the unity of federal Canada.

It should be noted, however, that the effect of leader appeal on party loyalties is not entirely transitory, but can lead to long-term realignments. Voters who are attracted to a party by the specific appeal of its leader may continue to vote for that party even when it acquires a new leader. Meisel has pointed out, for example, that Diefenbaker's influence on Prairie voting patterns in the 1950s and early 1960s has carried over into the 1970s, with many Prairie voters continuing to "follow John" by voting for his party.[36] Stanfield's tenure as Conservative Party leader may have a similar effect on Maritimes' voting habits, producing a body of Conservative support that will remain loyal even under the new party leader.

Third, because the Prime Minister's personal appeal will have contributed to the party's electoral success, his position is enhanced within the Cabinet, the caucus, and the party as a whole. Mackenzie King's security of tenure was based to a considerable extent upon the recognition given to his electoral skills, while the authority of Diefenbaker after 1958, and Trudeau after 1968, was greatly strengthened by the electoral debt the party owed to them personally. By the same token, of course, an electorally discredited leader becomes all the more of a liability to the party. As noted earlier in the chapter, however, the task of removing such a leader is much more difficult with the Convention system of selecting leaders than with a system of caucus selection. Thus if the leader is electorally successful the party can hardly afford to replace him, and if he is electorally unsuccessful it may be difficult to replace him if he is not prepared to retire quietly.

Finally, and most important for the themes explored in this book, the attention that is focused on the party leader through the Convention system and the nature of electoral campaigning, produces a situation in which the public sees the Prime Minister as the personification of the whole system of government. Public expectations of what he can *personally* achieve in office are inevitably raised, and policy successes or failures are attributed to his strengths or weaknesses. But can the Prime Minister exert such a degree of personal influence within the Cabinet, the caucus, and the machinery of government as a whole? Is there a clear gap between, on the one hand, the personalization of politics through the processes by which a Prime Minister comes to power, and on the other, the realities of political power in Canadian government? Almost certainly there is such a gap — but this general question will be examined in subsequent chapters.

NOTES

1. Sir Joseph Pope, *Memoirs of Sir John A. Macdonald*, (London: Edward Arnold, 1892), I: 319.
2. W. S. Wallace, *The Memoirs of Rt. Hon. Sir George Foster*, (Toronto: Macmillan, 1933), p. 81-2, and S. M. Scott "Foster on the Thomson-Bowell Succession", *Canadian Historical Review*, 1967, p. 275.
3. D. C. Thomson, *Alexander Mackenzie: Clear Grit* (Toronto: Macmillan, 1960), p. 147.
4. For a full analysis of the Convention system see J. C. Courtney, *The Selection of National Party Leaders in Canada* (Toronto: Macmillan, 1973).
5. Peter C. Newman, *Renegade in Power* (Toronto: McClelland and Stewart, 1963), p. 368.
6. Judy LaMarsh, *Memoirs of a Bird in a Gilded Cage* (Toronto: McClelland and Stewart, 1969), p. 336.
7. Courtney, *The Selection of National Party Leaders in Canada*, p. 163.
8. N. Ward, "The Liberals in Convention", *Queen's Quarterly*, 1958-9, p. 8.
9. L. LeDuc, "Party Decision-Making", *Canadian Journal of Political Science*, 1971, p. 109.
10. Courtney, *The Selection of National Party Leaders in Canada*, p. 63.
11. H. S. Ferns and B. Ostry, *The Age of Mackenzie King* (London: Heinemann, 1955), p. 312.
12. J. M. Beck, *Pendulum of Power* (Scarborough: Prentice-Hall, 1968), p. 288.
13. Newman, *Renegade in Power*, p. 50.
14. Ibid., p. 326.
15. J. Meisel, *The Canadian General Election of 1957* (Toronto: University of Toronto Press, 1962), p. 169.
16. Beck, *Pendulum of Power*, p. 415.
17. P. Regenstreif, *The Diefenbaker Interlude* (Toronto: Longmans, 1965), p. 74.
18. Ibid., p. 76.
19. J. Meisel, *Working Papers on Canadian Politics* (Montreal: McGill University Press, 1972), p. 31.
20. Ibid., p. 31. See also Peter Regenstreif's survey findings, reported in the *Toronto Daily Star*, June 19, 1968.
21. J. Pammett et al., *The 1974 Federal Election: A Preliminary Report* Carleton University Occasional Paper No. 4, p. 20.
22. Ibid., p. 24.
23. C. R. Winham and R. B. Cunningham "Party Leader Images in the 1968 Federal Election", *Canadian Journal of Political Science*, 1970, pp. 37-55.

24. Ibid., p. 55.
25. For a fuller statement of this view, and a critique of it, see P. N. Sniderman, H. D. Forbes, and I. Melser, "Party Loyalty and Electoral Volatility: A study of the Canadian Party System" *Canadian Journal of Political Science*, 1974, pp. 268-88. See also H. J. Jacek, "Party Loyalty and Electoral Volatility" *Canadian Journal of Political Science*, 1975, pp. 144-5; Jane Jenson, "Party Loyalty in Canada", *Canadian Journal of Political Science* 1975, pp. 543-52.
26. H. A. Scarrow "Distinguishing Between Political Parties— The Case of Canada", *Midwest Journal of Political Science,* 1965, pp. 61-76.
27. R. R. Alford, *Party and Society*, (Chicago: Rand McNally, 1963), p. 232.
28. See Jenson, *Canadian Journal of Political Science*, 1975, pp. 543-52.
29. J. R. Mallory, *The Structure of Canadian Politics*, Mount Allison University Publications, No. 4, 1959.
30. Sir Joseph Pope, ed., *Correspondence of Sir John A. Macdonald* (Toronto: Oxford University Press, 1921), p. 175.
31. Beck, *Pendulum of Power*, p. 80.
32. R. M. Dawson and N. Ward, *The Government of Canada* (Toronto: University of Toronto Press, 1963), p. 180.
33. Meisel, *Working Papers on Canadian Politics*, p. 159.
34. Peter C. Newman, *The Distemper of Our Times* (Toronto: McClelland and Stewart, 1968), p. 47.
35. Beck, *Pendulum of Power*, p. 404.
36. Meisel, *Working Papers on Canadian Politics*, p. 41.

4. Forming a Government: The Personnel and Machinery of Government

Once when signing a visitors' book Sir John A. Macdonald entered his occupation as that of "Cabinet-Maker" — a wry reference to the amount of time and energy that he was obliged to expend on the process of forming and re-forming a government.[1] At more than one stage when attempting to put together Canada's first Cabinet in 1867 Macdonald was in complete despair over the difficulties he faced, and was on the point of giving up the commission.[2] The problems involved in setting up the first government of Canada were, of course, particularly great. Macdonald was creating from scratch a completely new structure of federal government, and he had to bring together, and hold together, provincial leaders for whom federal politics was a completely new experience. No subsequent Prime Minister has had to perform quite such a pioneering task. Nevertheless, the process of creating a government remains a difficult one. Indeed, at least some of the difficulties faced by a modern Prime Minister are greater than those encountered by Macdonald a century ago. Because Canada today has more provinces, and is more socially complex, than in the nineteenth century, the task of producing a "representative" Cabinet is more difficult than it was. British Columbia, the Prairie provinces and Newfoundland have now to be accommodated, as well as the original provinces, and new immigrant groups expect recognition for their leaders. Further, the machinery needed to manage the government of Canada in the 1970s is vastly greater and more complex than was needed a century ago, or even thirty years ago.

A modern Prime Minister has to select a large personal staff as well as a Cabinet, and in an age of rapidly expanding government functions, he is likely to have to adapt the institutions of government that he inherits from his predecessor. The fundamental features of the Canadian Constitution, of course, are the same today as they were a century ago. Pierre Trudeau, like John A. Macdonald, serves within a Constitution that is parliamentary, federal, and monarchical. At various times there have been pressures for a change from a parliamentary to a presidential system, or for the abolition of the monarchy, or for the break-up of the federation, but such basic changes have been resisted. Nevertheless, there have clearly been major changes over the years in the ways in which the basic institutions of the Constitution operate. The relationship between the monarch, the Governor General, and the Prime Minister has changed over the years, with King's confrontation with Lord Byng in 1926 being the most dramatic event in the evolution of the relationship. The balance of power between Ottawa and the provincial governments has altered, not least as a result of arrangements worked out at Conferences between the federal Prime Ministers and provincial premiers. Within Parliament the balance of power between Senate and Commons, and within the Commons between Government and Opposition, has changed considerably over the years, with the reforms of the Trudeau government in the 1968-72 Parliament being important in this respect.[3]

Thus Prime Ministers have influenced in fundamental ways the basic institutions of the Constitution. At another level, Prime Ministers have changed major features of the machinery of government. New departments of state have been created, and the distribution of functions between departments has changed. The increase in the number of departments has produced changes in Cabinet machinery. Among these have been the acceptance of larger and larger Cabinets (14 members in July 1867 but 29 in July 1968), the use of a system of Cabinet committees to ease the work-load of the full Cabinet, and a growth in the number of ministerial posts outside the Cabinet, leading to the emergence of a clear distinction between the Cabinet and the ministry as a whole. Again, over the years Prime Ministers have built up an increasingly elaborate network of personal assistants and advisers in the Privy Council Office and the Prime Minister's Office.

These and other developments have produced major changes in the environment in which Prime Ministers, and their ministers, work. In this chapter an examination will be made of the twin processes of forming a team, and of building and adapting the machinery of government in which the team will operate, with particular emphasis on the factors that limit the Prime Minister's freedom of action.

SELECTING A TEAM

a. Constitutional and Party Considerations

The process of appointing Cabinet ministers has been described by one cynical political commentator as a "thoroughly unpleasant and discreditable business"[4] because of the variety of factors other than "mere merit" that the Prime Minister has to take into account in making his selection. What are these factors and how far do they limit the Prime Minister's freedom of choice? Mackenzie King, on forming his 1926 Cabinet, observed that:

> In the formation of a Cabinet an incoming Prime Minister is subjected to very distinct limitations and restrictions. He is not free to choose Ministers at his personal wish or will. Considerations of geography, of the size and total population of the Provinces, as well as economic, racial and religious considerations, of total and party membership in the House of Commons, and the special qualifications called for in the filling of certain portfolios, are all among the factors of which full account should be taken.[5]

There are two particularly fundamental restrictions upon his choice. The first of these is that ministers must be, or must become, members of the Prime Minister's party. The 1867 Macdonald government was a Liberal-Conservative coalition, and in 1917 Borden formed a short-lived Union government, but otherwise Canada has been ruled exclusively by single-party governments. The party membership requirement is fairly easily fulfilled, however, and in practice amounts to little more than the requirement that the potential minister should not be actively involved with any of the other parties. At a press conference after being appointed Minister of External Affairs in 1948, Lester Pearson was asked how long he had been a member of the Liberal Party: he replied, with characteristic honesty and gaucheness, "Since I was sworn in as a Minister a couple of hours ago."[6] Trudeau was also a relative newcomer to the Liberal Party when he became a minister, and he had even been an acknowledged NDP-supporter.

The second basic restriction is that ministers must be drawn from Parliament. This is not a statutory requirement, but it is an accepted unwritten constitutional principle. General McNaughton filled the key post of Defence Minister in 1944-45, even though he was not a member of either House, but this was exceptional, and he eventually resigned his post after twice failing to secure election to the Commons. Further, it is an accepted convention today that the vast majority of ministers must be members of the Commons rather than the Senate. In the nineteenth century it was common for Cabinets to contain at least three senators. Cabinets in this century, however, have rarely contained more than one or two senators, and for much of Diefenbaker's reign there was no minister in the Senate. E. N. Rhodes, who served as Minister of Finance in Bennett's government, was the last senator to fill one of the key posts, and now senators usually hold only non-departmental portfolios.

Although they must be members of Parliament, ministers need not have served a long parliamentary apprenticeship. Some evidence of this is provided in Table 4:1. Most newly formed Cabinets over the last fifty years have had a core of members (usually a half or a third) with ten or more years of parliamentary service, but they have all also contained a number of inexperienced ministers: the Trudeau, Pearson, Bennett, and 1926 King Cabinets were particularly short of ministers with long parliamentary service. Table 4:1 deals only with Cabinets when they were first formed, and does not take account of subsequent ministerial appointments. J. C. Courtney has calculated, however, that half of the Liberal ministers appointed in the 1921-70 period had less than five years parliamentary experience, and a third had less than a year (and this in a period of Liberal electoral dominance).[7]

The requirement that ministers must be members of Parliament is a characteristic of the form of parliamentary government that Canada has inherited from Britain. It should be noted, however, that West Germany, Italy, Belgium, Austria, Denmark, Ireland, Iceland, Finland, and Japan all operate parliamentary systems in which ministers *may*, but are not *obliged* to, be drawn from Parliament. While the Anglo-Canadian system of required parliamentary membership is "democratic", in the sense that ministers will have received electoral approval, it means equally that there is no ready access to ministerial posts for talented non-parliamentarians. This can be a particular disadvantage in a federal system, where potential ministers can be found at the provincial level of

Table 4:1

DISTRIBUTION OF CABINET MINISTERS ACCORDING TO
EXTENT OF PARLIAMENTARY EXPERIENCE

Prime Minister	Total Number of Ministers*	Number of Years of Parliamentary Experience				
		Less than one	1-3	4-6	7-9	Ten or more
		%	%	%	%	%
King, 1926	16	12.5	12.5	47.8	12.5	18.6
Bennett, 1930	16	37.5	—	12.5	18.6	31.3
King, 1935	14	14.4	7.2	7.2	21.6	50.0
St. Laurent, 1948	18	11.1	11.1	—	16.7	61.1
Diefenbaker, 1957	16	6.3	6.3	18.6	25.0	43.8
Pearson, 1963	24	37.8	4.2	8.4	16.8	33.6
Trudeau, 1968†	27	11.5	15.3	53.3	3.9	15.3

*Excluding Senators and the Prime Minister
†After 1968 general election

SOURCE: J. K. Johnson, ed., *Canadian Directory of Parliament* (Ottawa: Public Archives, 1968), and Government of Canada, *Guide to Canadian Ministries Since Confederation*, (2 vols.), (Ottawa: Public Archives, 1957 and 1967).

government. Outsiders, of course, can be found seats in the Commons through by-elections, but this is a cumbersome process, and by-elections often produce strange results (as illustrated by the Hochelaga by-election in 1975, when Pierre Juneau was defeated after having been appointed to the Cabinet). Appointment to the Senate remains as an alternative means of making non-parliamentarians eligible for office, and in 1962 Wallace McCutcheon was made a senator in order that he might join Diefenbaker's Cabinet. On the whole, however, little use has been made of the Senate for this purpose.

b. Practical Limitations

Within the two basic considerations of parliamentary and party membership, what other practical factors limit the Prime Minister's choice? For Mackenzie King, moral considerations were vital: "I was determined not to have men in the Cabinet who drank—that character must be the first essential."[8]

Such a sweeping prejudice, however, could never be applied in practice, given the variety of other factors that restrict the choice. In the first place, not all MPs will have ministerial potential. This is likely to be a particular problem if the government has only a small parliamentary majority (see Table 4:2). To ease the problem, the Prime Minister has to try to ensure, before an election, that potential ministers are adopted for safe seats. For the Conservative prime ministers this century the problem has usually been that of lack of *ministerial* experience among their MPs, in face of the party's long spells in Opposition. In 1911 they had been in Opposition for fifteen years, and Sir George Foster was the only potential minister with previous experience, while in 1957 they had been in Opposition for twenty-two years, and none of the Cabinet had any real federal executive experience.

Such difficulties will be compounded if, as is often the case, some of those who do possess the necessary talent decline to serve. Arthur Jones, Luther Holton, and Edward Blake all refused to join Mackenzie's Cabinet in 1873.[9] Blake later did join, after 104 Liberal MPs had petitioned him to do so, but he often threatened to resign, and eventually did. The Prime

Table 4:2

CABINET MINISTERS AS A PERCENTAGE OF CAUCUS

	Cabinet Ministers*	Govt. Party MPs	Cabinet Ministers as Percentage of MPs
King, 1926	16	128	12.5
Bennett, 1930	17	137	12.5
King, 1935	15	173	8.6
St. Laurent, 1948	19	193	9.8
Diefenbaker, 1957	17	112	15.1
Pearson, 1963	23	129	17.7
Trudeau, July 1968	28	155	18.0
Oct. 1972	29	109	26.6
Aug. 1974	28	141	19.8

*Excluding Senators

SOURCE: Government of Canada, *Guide to Candian Ministries Since Confederation,* (2 vols.), (Ottawa: Public Archives, 1957 and 1967) (up-dated from Keesing's Archives).

Minister can attempt to overcome a shortage of parliamentary talent by recruiting ministers from outside Parliament. Again, however, he may encounter refusals. Macdonald, attempting to recruit some youthful ministers in the 1880s, offered the post of Minister of Justice to D'Alton McCarthy, but McCarthy was not prepared to give up the income he was earning from his own legal practice.[10] Similarly, Walter Gordon declined to interrupt his financial career in 1954 to join St. Laurent's Cabinet,[11] while Lester Pearson declined to enter Parliament in 1946 to become Minister of External Affairs[12] (although, of course, Gordon and Pearson later did embark upon parliamentary and ministerial careers).

The Prime Minister's freedom of choice will also be limited by the fact that some individuals will have particularly strong claims to be included, whether the Prime Minister approves of them or not. A Prime Minister who has only just become party leader will have accumulated certain obligations to those who helped him to power. Mitchell Sharp had good claims to the post of External Affairs Minister in 1968, after contributing materially towards Trudeau's selection as party leader. In the interests of party unity the new Prime Minister may also need to accommodate those who opposed him in the leadership race. In 1957 Diefenbaker went so far as to complain that he had "to compose a Cabinet of my enemies!".[13] In 1968 Trudeau had to contend with the fact that Robert Winters and Paul Hellyer were in a position to divide the Liberal Party, while Joe Green and John Turner had gathered sufficient support at the Convention to make them influential figures within the party. In the event, Winters left federal politics, but Hellyer, Green, and Turner were offered, and accepted, important posts in Trudeau's new Cabinet.

The Prime Minister must also try to avoid giving rivals too powerful a Cabinet base. Some individuals, however, may be sufficiently powerful to be able to specify the actual post they will accept. In 1875 Mackenzie was obliged to offer the post of Justice Minister to Edward Blake, as a means of enticing him into the Cabinet and thereby ending intra-party strife.[14] Similarly, when Macdonald sought to persuade Sir John Thompson to join his Cabinet in 1885, to strengthen representation from Nova Scotia, the intermediary, Sir Charles Tupper, reported that "Thompson, I find, will go into your Cabinet if asked to do so as Minister of Justice—*not otherwise*."[15] Macdonald accepted this, but had then to persuade the incumbent Minister of Justice, Sir Alexander Campbell, to move to another department.

Provincial premiers who have "delivered" a province in a general election, or who are likely to be important figures for the next election, will have strong claims to a Cabinet post. In Laurier's Cabinet in 1896, the major posts of Finance, Justice, and Railways went to provincial premiers who were recruited specifically for these posts. Before the 1925 election Mackenzie King attempted, without success, to persuade Premier Charles Dunning of Saskatchewan to join the Cabinet in an effort to counter the Progressive Party's strength on the Prairies.[16] After the election Dunning indicated that he was now available, and King made him Minister of Railways, even though by then he was something of a threat to King's retention of the party leadership. In all, King appointed eight provincial premiers to his Cabinets, and J. C. Courtney argues that:

By pursuing extra-parliamentary notables with a vengeance, King effectively minimised the value of a Parliamentary career as an important consideration for future appointments to the Cabinet.[17]

Even if they are not themselves appointed, the views of provincial leaders will be important. Sir Leonard Tilley, on retiring from the Cabinet in 1885, effectively chose Sir George Foster as his successor, while Macdonald, in forming the 1867 Cabinet, went so far as to write to Tilley, then Premier of New Brunswick, saying:

I leave it to you to select an associate from New Brunswick. Is it to be Mitchell, Fisher, Wilmot, or who? Make up your mind, and bring him with you.[18]

No such sweeping offer is likely to be made today, but the influence of provincial leaders remains considerable.

A new party leader may inherit powerful ministers from his predecessor. Certainly, in the interests of Cabinet harmony the views of established ministers will have to be considered. In 1926 King wanted to appoint J. G. Gardiner, but he was a Saskatchewan rival of Charles Dunning, who had only recently joined the Cabinet, and the problem was that of reconciling the two men.[19] Pearson's attempts to bring Walter Gordon back into the Cabinet in 1967 were complicated by the difficulty of reconciling Gordon's views on American ownership of industry with the business sympathies of Mitchell Sharp and Robert Winters.[20] In the appointment of parliamentary secretaries the views of the departmental minister may be considered, although there is no guarantee of this (as Judy LaMarsh discovered in 1963 when she was presented with a parliamentary secretary of whom she did not particularly approve).[21]

The views of backbenchers will also have to be considered, and often a group of MPs will lobby the Prime Minister on behalf of a particular nominee. When Borden considered excluding Sir George Foster from the Cabinet in 1911, a group of his friends successfully pressed his claim.[22] Similarly in 1926 Lucien Cannon was appointed Solicitor General at the insistence of his Quebec colleagues.[23] Pressure can be applied from outside Parliament, and when the Liberals returned to power in 1963 some potential ministers organized constituents to send long telegrams to the Prime Minister, pressing their claims.[24] A Prime Minister at the head of a minority government has to assess the attitude of the third and fourth parties to his appointments. For all Prime Ministers, regardless of the size of their existing majorities, electoral reactions are vital, and after losing ground in English Canada at the 1972 election, Trudeau demoted a number of his French-Canadian colleagues.

c. Representational Factors

Perhaps most significantly of all, the Prime Minister's choice is limited by considerations of regional, ethnic, and religious representation. This particular fact of Canadian political life was recognized even before Confederation. During the 1865 Confederation Debates Christopher Durkin argued that:

> I think I may defy [the government] to show that the Cabinet can be formed on any other principle than that of a representation of the several provinces in that Cabinet . . . The Cabinet here must discharge all that kind of function, which in the United States is performed, in the federal sense by the Senate.[25]

Precisely how does the representative principle operate in practice? There are three main considerations. First, the Prime Minister has to achieve a balance of numbers between the regions on a rough "ministers-per-population" basis. In the 1867 Cabinet Cartier demanded four posts for Quebec, three of them to go to French Canadians.[26] As Ontario had a larger population it had to have one more post than this, with Nova Scotia and New Brunswick getting two each. The principle was extended as new provinces were added, and today each province, with the exception of Prince Edward Island, is normally allocated at least one Cabinet post. In the larger provinces distinctions will be drawn between localities. Representatives of Montreal, Quebec City, the English-speaking areas, and the eastern townships will normally be included among the ministers from Quebec. In 1875 Mackenzie made Joseph Cauchon President of the Privy Council, rather than the more able Wilfrid Laurier, because Cauchon was from Quebec City, which otherwise would not have had representation in the Cabinet.[27] The Ontario contingent will include representatives of Toronto and northern and eastern Ontario, while increasingly British Columbia has expected recognition of its regions in the allocation of portfolios.

The second consideration is that within the principle of provincial representation, a balance of ethnic and religious groups has to be achieved. In 1867 Cartier specified that three of Quebec's four posts should go to French Canadians. English-speaking Prime Ministers have usually sought a French-Canadian lieutenant. Cartier filled this role under Macdonald, and Ernest Lapointe and Louis St. Laurent under Mackenzie King, but not all prime ministers have been so well served. Mackenzie could not find an adequate successor to Dorion after his retirement, and Lester Pearson experimented with Lionel Chevrier, Maurice Sauvé, Maurice Lamontagne, Guy Favreau, and Jean Marchand. None of the Conservative prime ministers this century had a satisfactory lieutenant. Of the total number of Cabinet ministers to serve in the 1867-1965 period, 28 per cent were French Canadians, a figure which is remarkably close to the French-Canadian percentage of the population. Other ethnic distinctions may also be recognized. Early Cabinets would usually contain a balance of English, Scots, and Irish. In 1945 Mackenzie King appointed J. J. McCann, in preference to Paul Martin, largely as a gesture to the Irish community,[28] and in 1957 Diefenbaker included the Ukrainian Michael Starr. A balance of Protestants and Catholics will be sought, with some recognition also being given to the various Protestant denominations. This will overlap to some extent with the ethnic division, but at least one Catholic will normally be included among the Ontario representatives, and a Protestant among the Quebeckers. Overall, however, the Catholic half of the population can claim to have been under-represented over the years, in that it provided just a third of all Cabinet ministers in the first century of Confederation.

Finally, some departmental posts are associated with particular regions. A westerner usually gets the post of Minister of Agriculture, and a Maritimer the Fisheries post. In the early

Cabinets the Minister of Railways usually came from New Brunswick, as a large part of the only government railway network ran through the province. With the opening up of the west, however, the Railways portfolio came to be regarded as a westerner's post. The west also inherited from Ontario the post of Minister of the Interior. Ontario, as the most highly unionized province, has usually provided the Minister of Labour in recent years. Toronto, or English-speaking Montreal, usually provides the Ministers of Finance and Trade: the Trade post was not held by a French Canadian until 1968, and Finance until 1971. The post of Minister of Justice usually goes to Quebec, although under most Prime Ministers French Canadians have tended to get the less important posts. In 1968 Trudeau broke this pattern by giving a series of key posts (Treasury Board, Defence, Trade, National Revenue) to his Quebec colleagues, but in 1972, in face of an electoral setback in English Canada, he reduced the number of top posts held by French Canadians.

The detailed pattern of regional representation, of course, will vary from one Prime Minister to another. To some extent it will be governed by the number of MPs elected from each province, and from each region within the province. The Prime Minister has to try to ensure that his party's electoral strategy will enable it to obtain widely spread representation, although this is difficult to achieve. The Liberals have often had difficulty in getting adequate representation in the west. In 1921 Charles Stewart, the Liberal ex-Premier of Alberta, was recruited to the Cabinet through a seat in Quebec because there were no Liberal MPs elected in Alberta. Again, in 1935 there was only one Alberta Liberal MP (J. A. MacKinnon) and he duly entered the Cabinet as a minister without portfolio.[29] Under Pearson the Liberals had few western MPs, and Trudeau did only marginally better in 1968 before losing ground again in 1972. The Conservatives also faced an unusual problem with their western representation in 1911: R. B. Bennett and Charles Lougheed were the only Conservatives elected from Alberta in 1911, and as they were partners in the same law firm Borden felt he could make only one of them a minister.[30] More often, the Conservatives have been short of Quebec MPs,

Borden having only three after the 1917 election, and Meighen four in 1926. It, is precisely when representation is low, and the choice of ministers is limited, that it is desirable for the party to have a powerful Cabinet figure to reinforce its credibility in the area.

In St. Laurent's Cabinet ministers were allocated to clear and specific regional "spheres of influence".[31] Pearson and Trudeau did not devise quite so formal an arrangement, but the broad principle remains the same. The regional representative is expected to defend in Cabinet the interests of his province (or his region of the province) as well as of his department. Within overall Cabinet collective responsibility he has a special responsibility for his region, and is expected to defend its interests. He advises the Prime Minister about federal appointments in his area, and he acts as a channel of communication between the provincial party and government on the one hand, and the federal government on the other. From the federal government's point of view he acts as a sounding-board of local opinions. It remains arguable, however, who is most gratified by the system—the MPs concerned, the provincial government, the local activists, or the voters. Clearly, in practical terms there is much less need today than in 1867 to have regional representatives in the Cabinet, as there are so many other means through which provincial interests can be expressed. Federal-Provincial Conferences, meetings of premiers, representatives in the Prime Minister's Office, and intra-party machinery can all be used for this purpose, while modern mass communications and ease of travel mean that direct contacts with the federal government can be made with an ease that was inconceivable in 1867. In reality, Vancouver and Halifax today are little more remote from Ottawa than is Toronto. Nevertheless, the vital psychological factor remains, that justice is *seen* to be done if each province, locality, and ethnic and religious group receives a proportionate share of Cabinet posts. The principle of regional and group representation, then, remains significant for its own sake.

d. Representation and Merit

What are the consequences for the Prime Minister of having
to consider these several factors when forming his Cabinet?
The complexity of the Cabinet-making process means that it
can be a slow and wearing business. Macdonald almost gave
up the task of attempting to form the first Cabinet of Confederation,[32] while after completing his Cabinet in 1873
Mackenzie confessed that: "Although few Cabinets were ever
built so rapidly I was sick, sick, before it was done; really ill
in fact."[33]

Delays are likely if a party comes to power after a long spell
in Opposition. Laurier in 1896 managed to form his Cabinet
in two days, but Borden in 1911 took from September 25 to
October 10, and there was a public outcry as a result.[34] This
was exceptional, but it took Diefenbaker four days to complete
his list in 1957, and Pearson five days in 1963.

Merit is frequently sacrificed to the variety of other factors
that the Prime Minister has to consider. R. M. Dawson points
out that:

> Cabinet positions will undoubtedly be available for the best four
> or five of the Government's supporters; but the balance may
> be filled from the ranks of the party for reasons as varied as
> they are unconnected with parliamentary and administrative
> efficiency.[35]

The pattern was set in 1867, when Macdonald had to exclude
two of the Fathers of Confederation, D'Arcy McGee and Sir
Charles Tupper, to make way for Alexander Galt (as a representative of the Protestant minority in Quebec) and Edward
Kenny, who, according to Donald Creighton, ". . . happened
to be both a Nova Scotian and a Roman Catholic. He had
few other claims to distinction or to office; but in the circumstances he was apparently worth both the veterans, Tupper and
McGee."[36]

Again, Blair Neatby says of the appointment of Peter
Heenan to King's Cabinet in 1926 that:

> King knew that Heenan was "not an able man" but this dis-
> advantage was outweighed by the fact that he was a Roman
> Catholic, that as a locomotive engineer he seemed a suitable

Minister of Labour, and that his appointment would give representation to New Ontario.[37]

Loyal and able MPs who have been overlooked can sometimes be compensated with some other appointment within the Prime Minister's considerable range of patronage. Others, however, will remain on the backbenches as a possible source of disgruntled opposition: as has been remarked of an American president's power of patronage, "He will make one man ungrateful, and a hundred men his enemies for every office he can bestow."[38] Toronto-area MPs, for example, often form a sullen backbench bloc, disgruntled that their talents have been overlooked in order that representatives from other regions could be given ministerial posts.

The appointment of a number of relatively untalented ministers, of course, can help the Prime Minister to shine in relation to his colleagues, while the regional, religious, and ethnic bases of selection enhance the Prime Minister's own status as a truly national figure, surrounded by group-orientated colleagues. At the same time, the fact that the Cabinet's composition is based essentially on a variety of conflicting interests means that it becomes a difficult body for the Prime Minister to manage and hold together, with potential regional, ethnic, or religious divisions existing on many issues. On top of this, the difficulty of finding ministers to represent some regions or groups means that the person who is selected has an enhanced position within the Cabinet: the danger of dismissal is reduced for him, and his own threat of retirement becomes a powerful bargaining weapon. More important than these considerations, however, the nature of the selection process affects the overall efficiency of the Cabinet in two vital respects. First, the need to give representation to a wide variety of interests adds to the difficulty of keeping the Cabinet small and workman-like. Second, the subordination of merit to other factors reduces the Cabinet's value as a deliberative body, and makes it all the more important for the Prime Minister to have sources of information and advice other than the Cabinet. The fuller implications of these two factors will be considered in the second part of this chapter.

GOVERNMENT MACHINERY

a. An Unwieldy Cabinet

The selection of personnel is only one part of the process of forming a government. As noted in Chapter Two the Prime Minister has to be a skilled organization man as well as a recruiting officer, capable of providing an efficient institutional framework in which his team can operate. Over the years, Prime Ministers have found it necessary to appoint larger and larger Cabinets, with the greatest increase coming in the post-1945 period. In the nineteenth century the Cabinet usually contained about fifteen members, and for the first fifty years of this century it rarely contained more than twenty. Diefenbaker's Cabinet in 1957 had only seventeen members, but it had risen to twenty-three by the end of his term of office. Pearson's Cabinet had twenty-six members for most of the period. In April 1968 Trudeau reduced the number to twenty-five, but it rose to twenty-nine after the 1968 election, and to thirty in 1969. It was later reduced, but again reached thirty after the 1972 election.

The increased Cabinet size is a consequence of the new ministerial posts that have been created as the work of government has expanded. There were nine posts in Trudeau's Cabinet in 1972 that were not in St. Laurent's Cabinet in 1948. A body of thirty or so members is clearly too large to be an effective working committee. This, of course, can be to the Prime Minister's advantage in that a large unwieldy body is less likely to be able to challenge his personal ascendency than is a small workman-like body, in which each member can have a powerful voice. A large Cabinet, however, creates problems for the machinery of government, and means have to be found of achieving an efficient despatch of business. How have Prime Ministers dealt with these problems?

The most obvious and fundamental solution to the problems caused by the size of the modern Cabinet would be to reverse the trend by reducing the number of ministerial posts, either by reducing the scope of government or by the merger of two or three departments to create one "super-department" headed by one "super-minister". Another alternative would be to increase the number of posts outside the Cabinet, at the expense of Cabinet posts.[39] Such solutions involve major difficulties, however. The contraction of the scope of government is not immediately practical, while the creation of "super-departments" requires a degree of reorganization of the whole structure of government that no Prime Minister has yet felt able to tackle. What is more, the problem is compounded by the overriding need to achieve regional representation in the Cabinet. A comment by Laurier in the 1890s remains valid today:

> I have always holden to the view that to govern effectively a country like Canada with a population spread over such a very large territory, and with the necessity of giving Cabinet representation to all sections, no Prime Minister could undertake to reduce the cabinet. . . . Supposing you were to drop one cabinet minister, that would be an economy of $7,000, but if the reduction was from the province of Ontario, I do not believe the people of Ontario would be satisfied.[40]

Faced with such considerations, Prime Ministers have allowed the Cabinet to grow in size. At the same time, a system of Cabinet committees has been developed, particularly under Pearson and Trudeau, that has served to provide centres of decision-making away from the Cabinet as a whole. There are instances, of course, of ad hoc committees of the Cabinet being set up even in the nineteenth century. In August 1896 Laurier appointed a committee of Cabinet ministers to work out a solution to the Manitoba schools crisis,[41] and in 1897 he set up a committee to consider tariff policy.[42] Borden made use of committees to relieve the Cabinet's heavy work burden during the First World War. In 1915 a committee of five Cabinet ministers was formed to find a solution to the problems of marketing wheat in the wartime situation,[43] and in 1917 a committee was set up to examine a possible government take-over of the CPR.[44] Also, the coalition Cabinet in 1917 was divided into two sections, or "Committees", each with ten members and each chaired by the Prime Minister. One committee dealt with the prosecution of the war, and the other prepared plans for post-war reconstruction.[45]

A more elaborate Cabinet committee system emerged during the Second World War. An "Emergency Council" of the Cabinet was set up in 1938, and then in 1939 ten committees were formed, including the War Committee.[46] The War Committee had six members in 1939, and nine by 1945, with the ministers of Defence, Finance, and Munitions serving on it throughout the war. It met 345 times in all, and while it was nominally merely a committee of the Cabinet, it made most of the important decisions about the conduct of the war.[47] After the war it, and other committees set up in 1939, were replaced by four reconstruction committees.[48] In effect, however, the Committee system lapsed until revived by Pearson in the 1960s.[49]

Towards the end of his premiership, Pearson had ten standing committees of Cabinet, and a variety of special ad hoc committees.[50] Three of the standing committees (External Affairs and Defence, Federal-Provincial Relations, and the Sessional Committee) were chaired by the Prime Minister, and the other seven by senior ministers. Pearson introduced a Priorities and Planning Committee in 1967, but this was too late in his premiership for it to be effective.[51] Trudeau, however, developed this committee, and built on the system that Pearson had introduced. There were three main committees in the 1968-72 Parliament—Priorities and Planning set the government's priorities and attempted to integrate departmental policies; Federal-Provincial Relations dealt with government policies towards the provinces; the Treasury Board, a committee of the Privy Council rather than of the Cabinet, dealt with the budget and supervised the management of the public service.[52] Priorities and Planning, and Federal-Provincial Relations were chaired by the Prime Minister, and the Treasury Board by the President of the Treasury Board. There were various other standing committees, chaired by senior ministers, and some special committees which acquired a degree of permanence.

Under Trudeau the committees normally met weekly, with senior officials usually in attendance.[53] The system has served to reduce the frequency of full Cabinet meetings: the number fell from 139 under Pearson in 1966-67, to 70 or 80 per year under Trudeau in the 1968-72 Parliament, while the number of Cabinet committee meetings rose from 120 in 1966-67 to about 300 per year under Trudeau.[54] Committee membership broadens a minister's horizons by involving him in policy beyond his own immediate departmental or regional responsibility. There is a very real dilemma inherent in such a system, however. On the one hand, if real power passes from the Cabinet to its committees, a minister's involvement in general policy will be confined to those committees of which he is a member. This is a particular problem given that the principle of regional representation in the Cabinet as a whole cannot be reflected in every committee, and a region or group is likely to object if its Cabinet representative is excluded from a key committee. On the other hand, if each committee decision is re-examined in detail by the full Cabinet, there is an obvious duplication of effort. Trudeau has sought to avoid the extremes of these two dangers by operating the principle that the committee decisions are taken to be approved unless a minister raises an objection.[55] Committee recommendations are circulated to ministers prior to Cabinet meetings, and any minister who wishes to raise objections is given a chance to do so in Cabinet.[56]

The committee system adds to a minister's personal workload, however, and there is a danger that ministers will spend so long in committee that they may neglect their departmental and parliamentary duties. There is evidence that ministers have considerable difficulty in coping with the vast amount of paperwork produced by the committees.[57] In this, as in other respects, the development of the committee system has added to the complexity of the machinery of government. This, in its turn, makes it more difficult for the Prime Minister to exert personal control over the process of government. Another aspect of this problem will be considered in the next section.

b. The Prime-Ministerial Bureaucracy

What does the Prime Minister require in the way of secretarial, administrative, and personal assistance, and what machinery exists to provide it? There are three main functions that a prime-ministerial staff can perform. First, the Prime Minister requires secretarial and administrative assistants to undertake the day-to-day tasks of handling correspondence and memoranda, arranging appointments, and performing other routine clerical duties. These functions will be performed by a team of personal secretaries, administrative assistants, and clerical assistants. Second, he requires a supply of factual information about the affairs of government, to enable him to face his ministers from an informed base. If he is to be free from dependence on departmental civil servants, this factual information can only come from a private bureaucracy. Third, he requires a supply of informed political advice, to supplement his own judgment and keep him in touch with public and party opinion. In addition to these specifically prime-ministerial requirements, the Cabinet has to be serviced, machinery being required to prepare the agenda for meetings of the Cabinet and its committees, circulate papers, keep minutes, and supervise the implementation of Cabinet decisions.

When Alexander Mackenzie became Prime Minister in 1873 he did not even have a secretary to deal with his mail, and he answered all letters himself in long-hand, complaining "As letters come in bushels I have to answer them as fast as I can drive the pen."[58] Later he acquired a private secretary, and all Prime Ministers since then have had some form of basic secretarial and administrative assistance. Until the 1960s the Prime Minister usually held a departmental post, and thus had departmental machinery on which to draw. O. D. Skelton, for example, when Under-Secretary in the External Affairs Department, served as Mackenzie King's assistant, advising on domestic as well as foreign policy.[59] Prime Ministers have also usually had a close personal secretary, sometimes a woman. Alice Millar worked for R. B. Bennett in his law practice, and remained as his secretary when he became Prime Minister. Her influence was considerable, in that she was one of the few people to whom Bennett would turn for advice.[60] Mary Macdonald served Lester Pearson in a similar capacity, acting as "the Prime Minister's chamberlain, the guardian at the Monarch's door,"[61] insisting on handling all papers bound for the Prime Minister's desk.

Thus all Prime Ministers, apart from Mackenzie in his first few weeks in the post, have had some assistance. Since the 1930s, however, there has been a considerable growth in the number of prime-ministerial assistants. There have been two particular developments: the Privy Council Office (PCO) has been expanded to service the Cabinet and its committees, and the Prime Minister's Office (PMO) has been developed as a source of specifically political advice for the Prime Minister.

In 1938 Arnold Heeney became Principal Secretary to Mackenzie King, and then, in 1940, "Clerk and Secretary" to the Cabinet.[62] A Secretariat developed around him, and this was merged with the Chiefs of Staff Secretariat in 1944.[63] When the war ended, the Cabinet "inherited" Heeney and the Secretariat. In the immediate post-war period there were few real changes, with Heeney, and then Norman Robertson, J. W. Pickersgill, Robert Bryce, Gordon Robertson, and Michael Pitfield fulfilling a fairly passive political role because of the weight of their administrative duties. Heeney has since recorded the view that:

> I had little or no time to act as the personal staff officer to the Prime Minister, which I believe was the role which King had principally had in mind.[64]

Even the accession of Diefenbaker produced few changes. Bryce supervised the organization of Cabinet business, but Diefenbaker, suspicious of the "Liberal" civil service he inherited, insisted that his ministers were to be his political advisers, and made use of Royal Commission inquiries as an alternative to civil service advice.[65] In the Diefenbaker period the PCO was organized as a department with three main sections—the Cabinet-Secretariat to service the Cabinet, the Privy Council staff to deal with Orders-in-Council, and the Emergency Measures Organization set up in 1957 to prepare machinery that would operate in the event of nuclear war.[66]

Pearson, as part of his reorganization of Cabinet machinery, appointed four Assistant Secretaries to cover the four broad policy areas of the newly created Cabinet committees.[67] Trudeau expanded on this by creating more Assistant Secretaries for the Cabinet committees, and three new Deputy Secretaries, with a status between that of the Secretary and the Assistant Secretaries.[68] The three Deputy Secretaries headed sections of the PCO dealing with Federal-Provincial Relations, Operations, and Plans. The Plans section was designed to give Trudeau a policy input to the PCO machinery. A new planning unit was also set up for long-term policy thinking.[69]

Despite these developments, the Cabinet Secretary has remained very much an "organization man", concerned with ensuring that Cabinet machinery runs smoothly, rather than with providing the Prime Minister with political advice. Specifically *political* advice is provided by the staff of the PMO. This is not to say, of course, that Michael Pitfield or his predecessors have been political neuters. Gordon Robertson has described the situation as being that the PMO is "partisan, politically oriented, yet operationally sensitive" while the PCO is "non-partisan, operationally oriented yet politically sensitive".[70] Despite this political sensitivity of the PCO, however, both Pearson and Trudeau found it necessary to expand the size and activity of the PMO.

When the Liberals were in Opposition to the Diefenbaker government, Tom Kent served as Pearson's "civil service", drafting most of the party's policy proposals.[71] In 1963 he was brought into the PMO as "co-ordinator of programs", providing a more visible and directly political presence within the PMO than anything that had gone before. He was most active in the first two years of the Pearson government's life. He was succeeded by Marc Lalonde in 1966, who remained when Trudeau became Prime Minister in 1968.[72]

Trudeau made three principal changes in the machinery he inherited from Pearson. First of all, he increased considerably the size of the PMO. While Bennett in the 1930s had a staff of about a dozen, King, St. Laurent, and Diefenbaker about thirty, and Pearson about forty, Trudeau's staff in 1969 was sixty, and by 1972 was over ninety.[73] Second, he increased the appearance of the PMO as a private army with a specifically political role by making the staff "prime-ministerial servants" rather than civil servants. Sir Joseph Pope, O. D. Skelton, and Tom Kent had all acted as prime-ministerial advisers from civil service posts, and until 1968 almost all of the PMO staff were seconded from the civil service. Trudeau, however, broke these links with the civil service.[74] He also recruited a number of advisers from outside the government service entirely, including a team of constitutional lawyers to review the workings of the British North America Act.[75] Third, Trudeau created a number of new functions for the PMO. A Programme Secretary was appointed to provide a link with the party and its overall policy goals. After the 1974 election this post was replaced by a complete new secretariat entitled Policy, Plans, and Programmes. Regional desks were introduced in 1968 in an attempt to improve communications between the Prime Minister and the regions (although they were abandoned as a failure after the 1972 election).[76] A Nominations Division was set up under Francis Fox, to take charge of appointments to Crown Corporations. A more direct involvement by the Prime Minister in foreign affairs was sought through the appointment of Ivan Head as an external affairs adviser. These several developments increased the budget of the PMO from about $300,000 per year under Pearson, to almost $1,000,000 by 1970.[77]

To some extent the expansion of the PMO was a response to the increasing size and complexity of the machinery of government in the post-war period. There were other more personal factors involved, however. The planning of Pearson's day-to-day affairs, and of his travel arrangements in particular, had been casual and often chaotic, and Trudeau had to improve on this.[78] Trudeau himself was comparatively new to top-level politics, and thus had particular need of an elaborate intelligence service. Again, his theories of participatory democracy demanded good channels of communication with the electorate, and thus added to the need for sophisticated public-relations machinery in the television age. Above all, however, the expansion of the PMO was an attempt to strengthen the Prime Minister's specifically political sources of advice and information, as an alternative to the more traditional ministerial, departmental, and PCO sources. Although the PMO was discredited to some extent in the aftermath of the 1972 electoral setback, there were indications that it was reviving with the return to majority government in 1974.

Conclusions: Enhanced Prime-Ministerial Power?

The Cabinet and private office machinery over which a modern Prime Minister presides is altogether larger and more complex today than it was in the nineteenth century, or even before 1945. The Cabinet has increased in size, and a system of Cabinet committees has been developed, taking some of the work load, and some of the effective decision-making power, away from the Cabinet as a whole. The size and scope of the PCO has expanded, and a large PMO has emerged, providing the Prime Minister with a private bureaucracy. These developments underlie many of the arguments of those who claim that "Cabinet government" in Canada has now evolved into "prime-ministerial government". The unwieldy nature of the Cabinet; the development of the system of Cabinet committees with the most important of these chaired by the Prime Minister; the subordination of merit to other considerations in the Cabinet selection process—these factors are interpreted by some as indicating that the Cabinet as a whole has ceased to exercise effective influence and has joined the monarch (as Walter Bagehot expressed it) as a "dignified" rather than an "efficient" part of the Constitution. Equally, the creation of a prime-ministerial bureaucracy through the growth of the PCO and the PMO has led to parallels being drawn with the White House staff of an American president, and has thereby reinforced the arguments of those who claim that the Prime Minister has acquired "presidential" powers and status. Professor F. F. Schindeler, for example, as part of his general argument (referred to in Chapter One) that Canada has a prime-ministerial form of government, writes that:

> Given all the resources of the Office of the Prime Minister and of the Privy Council Office, . . . and the relationships that exist between these institutions and with the extra-parliamentary party, one is better able to assess the role of the Prime Minister in our system of government. Elected by a national party conference, supported by a majority in Parliament who are largely dependent upon him for their continued existence in office, supported by a Cabinet selected by himself and holding office at his pleasure, able to call upon the resources of the well trained and well paid professional staff in the Cabinet Secretariat, informed and advised by the extra-parliamentary party

hierarchy and assisted by an elite personal staff, the Prime Minister occupies a position of power in some ways unrivalled even by the President of the United States.[79]

Undoubtedly, a strong PMO gives the Prime Minister a degree of independence from civil service information and ministerial advice: it enables him to compete with his colleagues more effectively than would otherwise be the case. The division of responsibilities between the PMO and the PCO is also to the Prime Minister's advantage in that it prevents either one from becoming all-powerful: the blurred boundaries of their respective responsibilities allow the Prime Minister to divide and rule by playing one off against the other.

Also, his patronage power is increased by the large number of PMO posts that are to be filled. A number of important qualifications need to be made, however, to this picture of increased prime-ministerial authority. In the first place, the size of the PMO under Trudeau can be misleading. Only twenty of the ninety PMO staff in 1972 were "advisers", and the remainder were secretaries or comparatively junior administrative or clerical assistants.[80] The Correspondence Division, to handle the Prime Minister's mail, had about forty members, twice the number that Pearson had (and forty times the number that Mackenzie had a century earlier). Each adviser is involved only in his own policy area, and has only limited research and planning assistance, so that in-depth policy analysis cannot be achieved.[81] Nor are the advisers recruited solely on the basis of merit, as even appointments at this personal level have to be made with a view to the balance between the regions.[82]

Again, the PMO is far from being the Prime Minister's only source of advice, and he also still looks to the more traditional sources ministers, civil servants, MPs, and a range of individuals and groups outside the machinery of government. Perhaps as an indication of where real power still lies, Marc Lalonde resigned from the PMO in 1972 to enter Parliament and the Cabinet (where he was not placed particularly well in the ministerial hierarchy).[83] In the sphere of policy initiation the PMO is overshadowed by the Department of Finance, the Treasury Board, and the PCO: while the PMO concentrates on the issues with which the Prime Minister is currently involved, these other bodies concern themselves with the whole range of government.

The creation of a prime-ministerial bureaucracy may merely serve to duplicate advice the Prime Minister receives. A private bureaucracy is also liable to cause resentment among ministers, civil servants, and MPs. Ivan Head, as Trudeau's chief foreign policy adviser in the PMO, has claimed that: "I don't think it hurts the mandarins to know that the Prime Minister has people in his office with both experience and ability to challenge what comes up."[84] Perhaps not, but the mandarins undoubtedly resent such alternative centres of power. Certainly in the first years of Trudeau's premiership, when the role of the PMO advisers was not always made clear, a lot of ill feeling was aroused within the civil service.

Two particular points need to be emphasized by way of conclusion. First, precisely because the machinery of government is now larger and more complex than it was in the past, the task of managing it is all the more difficult. Institutions designed to streamline a process can manufacture their own delays, in that the more agencies and posts that are created, the more desks and in-trays there are to ensnare memoranda and correspondence. As G. B. Doern points out: "The exercise of power is related to the degree of uncertainty and discretion that characterises the relationship between political actors".[85] The growth of the PCO and the PMO, and the development of the Cabinet committee system, add a further element of rigidity to the machinery of federal government in Canada, and future Prime Ministers will face the problems of controlling not only ministers and civil servants, but also the occupants of posts in the PCO and PMO.

Second, the existence of a streamlined Cabinet committee system served by the PCO, and of a large PMO, still does not enable a modern Prime Minister to enjoy any greater personal control over the process of government than did nineteenth-century or pre-war Prime Ministers. Because of the vast growth that has taken place in the extent of the activities of the federal government, a modern Prime Minister requires a large machine and support staff merely to maintain his relative position within the machinery of government. Indeed, the scope and technical nature of the tasks of government in the 1970s is such that Trudeau, even with a personal staff of ninety, can exert less of a personal control over the decision-making process than could R. B. Bennett with a staff of a dozen. The precise nature of the relationship between the Prime Minister and his ministerial colleagues, however, needs to be examined in more detail, and this is done in the next chapter.

NOTES

1. W. S. Wallace, *The Memoirs of the Rt. Hon. Sir George Foster* (Toronto: Macmillan, 1933), p. 54.
2. For details of the formation of the first Cabinet see Sir Joseph Pope, *Memoirs of Sir John A. Macdonald* (London: Arnold, 1894), I: 329-31.
3. See particularly Robert J. Jackson and Michael M. Atkinson, *The Canadian Legislative System* (Toronto: Macmillan, 1974), Chs. 5 and 6.
4. Paul Bilkey, *Persons, Papers and Things* (Toronto: 1940), p. 140.
5. H. B. Neatby, *William Lyon Mackenzie King, 1924-32: The Lonely Heights* (Toronto: University of Toronto Press, 1963), p. 172.
6. Lester Pearson, *Memoirs 1897-1948: Through Diplomacy to Politics* (London: Gollancz, 1973), p. 296.
7. J. C. Courtney, *The Selection of National Party Leaders in Canada* (Toronto: Macmillan, 1973), p. 157. Some of the consequences of lack of parliamentary experience were discussed above, p. 16.
8. Quoted in J. C. Courtney, "Prime Ministerial Character: An Examination of Mackenzie King's Political Leadership", *Canadian Journal of Political Science*, 1976, p. 94.
9. D. C. Thomson, *Alexander Mackenzie: Clear Grit* (Toronto: Macmillan, 1960), pp. 170-2.
10. D. Creighton, *John A. Macdonald* (Toronto: Macmillan, 1955-6), II: 390.
11. D. Smith, *Gentle Patriot: A Political Biography of Walter Gordon* (Edmonton: Hurtig, 1973), p. 30.
12. Pearson, *Memoirs*, p. 293.
13. Peter Stursburg, *Diefenbaker: Leadership Gained, 1956-62* (Toronto: University of Toronto Press, 1975), p. 70.
14. Thomson, *Alexander Mackenzie*, p. 236.
15. Sir Joseph Pope, ed., *Correspondence of Sir John A. Macdonald* (Toronto: Oxford University Press, 1921), p. 351.

16. David E. Smith, *Prairie Liberalism* (Toronto: University of Toronto Press, 1975), pp. 182-3.
17. Courtney, *CJPS*, 1976, p. 95.
18. Pope, *Memoirs of Sir John A. Macdonald*, p. 329.
19. Neatby, *William Lyon Mackenzie King*, p. 118.
20. Smith, *Gentle Patriot*, p. 295.
21. Judy LaMarsh, *Memoirs of a Bird in a Gilded Cage* (Toronto: McClelland and Stewart, 1969), p. 57.
22. Wallace, *The Memoirs of Rt. Hon. Sir George Foster*, pp. 154-61.
23. Neatby, *William Lyon Mackenzie King*, p. 174.
24. LaMarsh, *Memoirs*, p. 47.
25. Confederation Debates, 1965, p. 497.
26. Pope, *Memoirs of Sir John A. Macdonald*, p. 330.
27. Thomson, *Alexander Mackenzie*, p. 253.
28. R. M. Dawson, "The Cabinet: Position and Personnel", *Canadian Journal of Economics and Political Science*, 1946, pp. 261-81.
29. Ibid., p. 266.
30. Ernest Watkins, *R. B. Bennett: A Biography* (London: Secker and Warburg, 1963), p. 79.
31. LaMarsh, *Memoirs*, p. 140.
32. Pope, *Memoirs of Sir John A. Macdonald*, pp. 329-31.
33. Thomson, *Alexander Mackenzie*, p. 172.
34. Bruce Hutchison, *Mr. Prime Minister 1867-1964* (Don Mills: Longmans, 1964), p. 151.
35. Dawson, *CJEPS*, 1946, p. 270.
36. Creighton, *John A. Macdonald*, I: 474.
37. Neatby, *William Lyon Mackenzie King*, p. 173.
38. John Adams' remarks on hearing of the election of his son, John Quincy Adams, to the Presidency in 1824.
39. A. Alexander, "Canada's Parliamentary Secretaries: Their Political and Constitutional Position", *Parliamentary Affairs*, 1966-7, pp. 248-57.
40. O. D. Skelton, *Life and Letters of Sir Wilfrid Laurier* (London: Oxford University Press, 1922), II: 5.
41. Ibid., p. 13.
42. Ibid., p. 52.
43. H. Borden, ed., *Robert Laird Borden: His Memoirs* (London: Macmillan, 1938), p. 525.
44. Ibid., p. 775.
45. Ibid., p. 758.
46. A. D. P. Heeney, "Cabinet Government in Canada: Developments in the Machinery of the Central Executive", *Canadian Journal of Economics and Political Science*, 1946, pp. 283-

301. See also J. L. Granatstein, *Canada's War* (Toronto: Oxford University Press, 1974).

47. Ibid., p. 288.

48. Ibid., p. 290.

49. See, for example, P. C. Newman, *Renegade in Power* (Toronto: McClelland and Stewart, 1963), p. 343.

50. For details of membership see P. C. Newman, *The Distemper of Our Times* (Toronto: McClelland and Stewart, 1968), p. 201, and B. Fraser, "Your Guide to the New Split Level Cabinet", *Maclean's*, April 4, 1964, p. 18.

51. G. B. Doern and P. Aucoin, *The Structures of Policy Making in Canada* (Toronto: Macmillan, 1971), p. 64.

52. See T. A. Hockin, ed., *Apex of Power: The Prime Minister and Political Leadership in Canada* (Toronto: Prentice Hall, 1971), and A. W. Johnson "The Treasury Board of Canada and the Machinery of Government in the 1970's", *Canadian Journal of Political Science*, 1971, pp. 346-66.

53. R. J. Van Loon and M. S. Whittington, *The Canadian Political System* (Toronto: McGraw-Hill, 1971), p. 382.

54. A. Westell, *Paradox: Trudeau as Prime Minister* (Scarborough: Prentice-Hall, 1972), p. 11.

55. B. Thordarson, *Trudeau and Foreign Policy* (Toronto: Oxford University Press, 1972), p. 90.

56. Walter Stewart, *Shrug: Trudeau in Power* (Toronto: New Press, 1972), pp. 162-72.

57. Westell, *Paradox: Trudeau as Prime Minister*, pp. 111-13; LaMarsh *Memoirs*, pp. 259-60.

58. Thomson, *Alexander Mackenzie: Clear Grit*, p. 174.

59. P. C. Newman, "Reflections on a Fall from Grace", *Maclean's*, January 1973, p. 21.

60. Watkins, *R. B. Bennett: A Biography*, pp. 168-9.

61. P. C. Newman, *The Distemper of Our Times*, p. 67.

62. Arnold Heeney, *The Things That Are Caesar's* (Toronto: University of Toronto Press, 1972), pp. 42, 63.

63. Heeney, *CJEPS*, 1946, p. 289.

64. Heeney, *The Things That Are Caesar's*, p. 79.

65. Doern and Aucoin, *The Structures of Policy Making in Canada*, p. 45, and Newman, *Renegade in Power*, p. 83.

66. W. E. D. Halliday, "The Executive of the Government of Canada", *Canadian Public Administration*, 1959, pp. 229-41.

67. Doern and Aucoin, *The Structures of Policy Making in Canada*, p. 48.

68. Stewart, *Shrug: Trudeau in Power*, p. 178.

69. Thordarson, *Trudeau and Foreign Policy*, pp. 86-9.

70. Ibid., p. 86.

71. Smith, *Gentle Patriot*, p. 136.

72. Newman, *The Distemper of Our Times*, p. 66.
73. Stewart, *Shrug: Trudeau in Power*, p. 178, and Thomas D'Aquino, *The Prime Minister's Office—Catalyst or Cabal* (paper presented to UK-Canada Colloquium, Montreal, August 1973).
74. Thordarson, *Trudeau and Foreign Policy*, p. 87.
75. Westell, *Paradox: Trudeau as Prime Minister*, p. 24.
76. Ibid., p. 68.
77. Ibid., p. 115.
78. Ibid., p. 114.
79. Hockin, *Apex of Power*, p. 48.
80. D'Aquino, *The Prime Minister's Office*, p. 4.
81. Westell, *Paradox: Trudeau as Prime Minister*, p. 120.
82. D'Aquino, *The Prime Minister's Office*, p. 22.
83. Westell, *Paradox: Trudeau as Prime Minister*, p. 116.
84. Thordarson, *Trudeau and Foreign Policy*, p. 88.
85. Doern and Aucoin, *The Structures of Policy Making in Canada*, p. 74.

5.   Prime Minister
        and Cabinet
        at Work

There are four main theoretical models of the way in which policy decisions are made in parliamentary-Cabinet systems of government. Two of the models imply a collective decision-making process, and two imply individual decision-making.

1. Individual decision-making.
   a) Prime-ministerial model: Decisions are taken by the Prime Minister, with individual ministers, and the Cabinet collectively, quietly acquiescing.
   b) Ministerial model: On the principle of departmental independence, each minister in his own subject area is given vast freedom from Cabinet and prime-ministerial control. A variation of this is the bureaucratic model, whereby the minister's power is exercised by his departmental officials.

2. Collective decision-making.
   a) Cabinet model: The Cabinet, under the Prime Minister's largely passive chairmanship, collectively makes key decisions to which departmental ministers accede.
   b) Inner-group model: Decisions are made by a sub-group of the Cabinet (be it a Cabinet Committee, a formally constructed Inner Cabinet, or an informal group of ministers who have a special interest in a particular issue) with the rest of the Cabinet performing a largely nominal role.

In very general terms, it would be possible to classify countries with parliamentary-Cabinet systems of government according to the model which is most characteristic of their decision-making processes. Two basic limitations on such a classification should be noted, however. In the first place, the four models are not mutually exclusive. The nature of the decision-making process will vary to some extent from issue to issue, and under any Prime Minister each model will apply at one time or another. With comparatively minor matters of "house management", for example, each department will be largely free from Cabinet intervention, while some matters, such as the timing of the general election, will be decided by the Prime Minister alone. On some other matters the Prime Minister will seek guidance from a small group of ministers, while on others the collective voice of the whole Cabinet will be the determining factor.

Second, although it may be possible to say that in a particular country at a particular time one model is more pervasive than the others, the pattern is liable to change through time. Long-term trends within the system of government may produce a change from one model to another. Even in the short-term, however, some ministers and Cabinets will be more passive than others, while some Prime Ministers will be more likely than others to take decisions on their own, with only minimum consultation with Cabinet colleagues. Among the variables that affect this will be the ability, status, and inclination of ministers on the one hand, and of the Prime Minister on the other, and the nature of the issues with which they are faced.

Given these considerations, what can be said of minister-Prime Minister-Cabinet relations within the Canadian federal decision-making process? In particular, how far is it the case that the prime-ministerial model operates in Canada? To determine this it is necessary to try to assess how far ministers enjoy freedom from prime-ministerial control within their own subject area, how much influence is wielded by the Cabinet as a collective body, and how much is wielded by inner groups of one type or another within the Cabinet. These issues will be dealt with in this chapter, together with an examination of the difficulties the Prime Minister faces in his attempts to hold the team together.

THE PRIME MINISTER AND HIS MINISTERS

a. Ministerial Independence

To what extent does a Prime Minister concern himself with the details of departmental policy? Of all Canadian prime ministers R. B. Bennett was probably the most inclined to involve himself in the minutiae of each department's affairs. He regularly dealt with civil servants over their minister's head, and he was liable to discuss any item of business with relatively minor officials.[1] Bennett also generally ignored his colleagues in public declarations of policy. Prior to the 1935 election, for example, he seriously embarrassed his ministers, and the Conservative Party as a whole, by announcing, purely on his own initiative, a controversial new reform program.[2]

Alexander Mackenzie also tended to involve himself in the details of departmental business, and frequently answered questions in the House, or spoke in debates, on his ministers' behalf. As his biographers acknowledge:

> The effect of this upon the House and the country was unfavourable to his Cabinet as a whole, as it deprived his Government of that political confidence which the well-known individual ability of each Minister necessarily produces.[3]

Sir Wilfrid Laurier's relationship with his ministers was very different. According to O. D. Skelton:

> As Prime Minister Sir Wilfrid was not a hard task-master. He did not intervene in the details of the administration of his colleagues. He believed in giving every Minister wide latitude and large responsibility.[4]

Lester Pearson also interpreted his role as being that of leaving ministers in charge of their own departmental business, with a prime-ministerial initiative being exercised only when policies went awry.[5] The controversial decision to unify the armed forces, for example, was finally taken by the Minister of Defence,[6] Paul Hellyer. On occasions, however, Pearson took firm action without consulting his colleagues. For example, he personally decided to introduce the flag issue in 1964, and did not broach the subject with the Cabinet, the caucus, or his personal advisers until he had made his decision.[7] Again, he personally negotiated an agreement with the Government of Quebec in 1964 about the adoption of the Canada Pension Plan.[8] The departmental minister concerned (Judy LaMarsh) was not consulted, but was merely informed that an agreement had been made. Also, Pearson saw himself as having a "special relationship" with the civil service, and on occasions dealt directly with civil servants over the head of the departmental minister.[9] In general, however, this was untypical of Pearson's normal prime-ministerial style. For the most part his government was characterized by policies being made by ministers individually, or by the Cabinet collectively, rather than by firm prime-ministerial initiatives. One consequence of this was that Pearson was rarely in command of a series of minor crises, and by 1968, when he was about to retire, his ministers were openly squabbling as they sought advantages in the race for the succession.[10]

Trudeau has tended to involve himself with federal-provincial relations, regional development, Quebec and constitutional issues, and certain aspects of foreign policy.[11] The outcome of the general review of Canada's NATO role, that the Trudeau government undertook soon after taking office, closely reflected Trudeau's personal views on the issue.[12] The decision to grant diplomatic recognition to Communist China was taken by the Cabinet, with the Department of External Affairs working within the guide-lines laid down by the Cabinet. During the Quebec crisis in October 1970, Trudeau worked very closely with John Turner, the Minister of Justice. The decision to allow the Public Order legislation to lapse in April 1971, however, was made at Turner's insistence, and against Trudeau's own inclination to continue the emergency measures.[13]

Ultimately, of course, the Prime Minister can dispense with ministerial and Cabinet "interference" by taking charge of a department himself, perhaps even prohibiting Cabinet discussion of its affairs. The early Prime Ministers usually held at least one departmental portfolio. During his first spell as Prime Minister, Macdonald was Minister of Justice and Attorney General, as was Sir John Thompson during his premiership. For part of his second term as Prime Minister, Macdonald served as Minister of the Interior, and then as Minister of

Railways,[14] while Mackenzie was Minister of Public Works throughout his premiership. In the nineteenth century the Prime Minister was solely responsible for foreign affairs, and although a Department of External Affairs was created in 1909,[15] the Prime Minister normally held the post of External Affairs Minister until the 1940s. King would not even permit Cabinet discussion of foreign policy, and personally made a number of foreign-policy decisions without any reference to his colleagues. He personally decided the role that Canada would play in the Italian crisis of 1935, and the Munich crisis of 1938,[16] while a joint Board of Defence for Canada and the U.S.A. was created at a secret personal meeting between King and President Roosevelt in August 1940.[17] Even after appointing St. Laurent to the post of Secretary of State for External Affairs in 1946, King continued to answer many of the parliamentary questions on foreign affairs and to play the main role in many foreign-affairs debates.[18] In turn, St. Laurent continued to take a close interest in foreign affairs when he became Prime Minister, with Lester Pearson as his External Affairs Minister.[19] Diefenbaker held the External Affairs post himself for the first three months of his premiership, and again for the three months after Sidney Smith's death in 1959. When he did have an External Affairs Minister he was reluctant to take his advice, and he was suspicious of the "Liberal" civil servants in the External Affairs Department.[20] In 1957 Diefenbaker personally decided to accept the NORAD concept without consulting the Cabinet or the officials of the External Affairs Department.[21]

For two years in the 1930s Bennett held the two key posts of Finance and External Affairs. Mackenzie King gained some amusement from the spectacle in Parliament of "Bennett handling all the estimates and his Ministers sitting around him like frightened children . . . ."[22] The Conservatives, of course, had been out of office for all but three months of the previous nine years, and Bennett had few experienced MPs from whom to draw his ministerial team. Nevertheless, this accumulation of key offices typifies Bennett's prime-ministerial style. No Prime Minister since Bennett has taken on such a heavy load. Diefenbaker was External Affairs Minister for only a few months, while St. Laurent, Pearson, and Trudeau held no departmental posts (apart from the "caretaker" period of April to June 1968 when Trudeau served as Minister of Justice and Attorney General). In the 1921-57 period, and occasionally before 1921, the Prime Minister was also President of the Privy Council, but Diefenbaker, Pearson, and Trudeau gave even this post to someone else. For the most part, recent Prime Ministers have chosen to follow Laurier's practice of remaining free from departmental duties in order to fill the role of co-ordinator-in-chief of government policy.[23]

b. Influencing Ministers

In his role as supreme policy co-ordinator, how much influence does the Prime Minister exercise? In particular, what strategies can he use to try to ensure that in a policy dispute his point of view will prevail, rather than that of the departmental minister? Faced with a particularly difficult minister the Prime Minister can, ultimately, "make him an offer he cannot refuse", and either dismiss him from the team or demote him to a less attractive post. This extreme weapon, however, cannot be used lightly. The Prime Minister's main concern is to hold the team together, not to break it up, and (as is noted elsewhere)[24] there are numerous practical limitations on the Prime Minister's freedom to hire and fire. Fortunately, the Prime Minister has at his disposal a number of more subtle means of persuasion. He can, for example, approach the minister on a private, personal basis and make a general appeal to him to comply with the prime-ministerial view out of personal loyalty (perhaps on the strength of past favours) or in the interests of Cabinet unity. Again, he can appeal to the minister on the basis of "the party interest" or "the national interest", drawing on his prime-ministerial prestige as the party and national leader.

As well as such general appeals the Prime Minister can use a variety of more specific "sticks" and "carrots" to tempt or bully the minister into accepting the prime-ministerial viewpoint. One of the major rewards that the Prime Minister can offer is the prospect of promotion to a more attractive ministerial post. Like the ultimate threat of dismissal, of course, this tactic is limited by the several practical restrictions that exist on the Prime Minister's freedom of appointment, and by the fact that no Prime Minister can afford to indulge in too frequent ministerial reshuffles. Prime-ministerial patronage, however, extends beyond purely ministerial appointments, and one of the variety of posts in the public service that are at the Prime Minister's disposal can be offered to the minister or to one of his nominees. Again, policy concessions can be offered, with prime-ministerial backing on one issue being offered in return for the minister's acquiescence on another. The fact that the minister is also a regional and group representative means that the Prime Minister can offer rewards, be it patronage or policy, at the provincial or constituency level, in return for a ministerial concession on departmental policy.

The main punishments at the Prime Minister's disposal are the reverse of these rewards: he can decline to promote the minister or to support his other policy initiatives, or to give appointments to his nominees. If the minister's parliamentary seat is held by only a slender majority, the Prime Minister can even threaten to starve him of party funds and attention in the next election campaign. By such means considerable pressure can be brought to bear upon a minister. If these private appeals, threats, and promises fail to move the minister, the Prime Minister can draw other ministers into the dispute and attempt to use the collective voice of the Cabinet to persuade the minister to give way. The use of the Cabinet as a forum for settling such ministerial disputes needs to be looked at in some detail.

THE PRIME MINISTER AND HIS CABINET

a. Cabinet Deliberations

What is the Prime Minister's relationship with his Cabinet? It is "the Prime Minister's Cabinet" in the sense that he selects its members and is responsible for the general organization and conduct of its affairs. The Cabinet has no legal status of its own, and its formal powers are exercised through the Privy Council. In effect it is the "operative part of the Council".[25] Cabinet meetings are normally held in the Parliament buildings; in the Centre Block when Parliament is in session, or in somewhat cramped conditions in the East Block during the recess.[26] Occasionally, meetings may be held elsewhere. When Macdonald was ill in 1881, for example, the Cabinet met at his home,[27] and Diefenbaker and Pearson also held occasional meetings at their residences.[28] Such gatherings away from Parliament Hill, however, are exceptional, and the normally close physical proximity of the Cabinet to the Chamber of the Commons is symbolic of the principle of prime-ministerial and governmental responsibility to Parliament.

While the venue of Cabinet meetings is largely unchanging, the frequency and length of meetings has varied considerably from one Prime Minister to another. In the last full year of the St. Laurent government (1956), the Cabinet met 91 times, but under Diefenbaker in 1959 it met 164 times.[29] Macdonald's Cabinet usually met each afternoon when Parliament was in session.[30] Under Pearson the Cabinet normally met on Tuesday and Thursday mornings for three hours or so.[32] Under Trudeau it has usually met once per week, with an additional monthly "political Cabinet", when ministers and party officials would assess the government's electoral standing.[33] Trudeau's Cabinet meetings usually last from 10:00 a.m. to 1:00 p.m., although they sometimes continue until the House meets at 2:00 p.m.[34] Occasionally there may be longer sessions. In March 1959, for example, a special gathering of the Cabinet, to decide on NATO policy, lasted the whole of one weekend.[35] After the 1963 election, Pearson's Cabinet sat all day and every day, drawing up its legislative program.[36] There will also be extended sessions in crisis situations. At the height of the crisis over the Spencer affair in 1966, for example, the Cabinet met daily for a week or more.[37] In October 1897 there was a two-day session of Laurier's Cabinet to decide the nature of Canada's participation in the Boer War,[38] while on August 2 and 3, 1914 the Cabinet sat in almost constant session.[39]

The agenda for each Cabinet meeting is prepared by the PCO under the Prime Minister's supervision.[40] In effect there are two agendas, the first listing the four or five major items to be considered at the meeting, together with the names of those who have indicated that they wish to speak on the issue, and the second listing the twenty or thirty decisions that have been taken by Cabinet committees. The agendas are circulated to Cabinet members before the meeting, together with relevant documents. Ministers who wish to raise points about agenda items are asked to circulate explanatory memoranda.[41] Such an orderly system helps towards an efficient conduct of Cabinet business, but restricts the chairman's ability to orchestrate the meeting. Before the creation of the Cabinet Secretariat in 1940, the informal and somewhat haphazard conduct of meetings gave the Prime Minister considerable control over Cabinet deliberations. In the absence of a formal agenda, Mackenzie King would begin Cabinet meetings by raising the matters he wanted to have discussed, and would then invite ministers, in the order that suited *him* best, to raise matters they wished.[42] Given inevitable pressures of time it was often possible for King to reduce the amount of attention accorded to particular items, or perhaps exclude them entirely from consideration. Such manipulation is much more difficult now that there are formal agendas and papers for discussion, circulated in advance of meetings.

In Cabinet meetings the Prime Minister, as chairman, sits at one end of the oval table in the same red leather chair that was used by John A. Macdonald. His ministers are ranged round the table in order of precedence based upon their length of service in the Cabinet, with the longest-serving ministers sitting closest to the Prime Minister. There is a clear irony in this arrangement, in that the Prime Minister is not necessarily the longest-serving minister. Liberal Prime Ministers in particular have often been surrounded by more experienced colleagues, and in April 1968 three-quarters of Trudeau's ministers had more Cabinet experience than he had.[43]

The Prime Minister's role as chairman is inevitably a difficult one, given the conflicting interests among his ministers. J. W. Dafoe has pointed to Wilfrid Laurier's difficulties in this respect:

> As a question grew and ramified, reaching out into department after department, Laurier was sometimes so strained and wracked by the mere work of peacemaking that the issue itself was obscured for him.[44]

Israel Tarte was a major source of conflict in Laurier's

Cabinet, while Charles Fitzpatrick (a Quebec Catholic) and Clifford Sifton (a Prairie Protestant) clashed regularly because of their religious, provincial, and personality differences.[45] All Prime Ministers face these sorts of problems, which are inevitable when Cabinets contain powerful sectional leaders. In his 1921 Cabinet, King often had to mediate between Charles Murphy, a fervent Laurier Liberal, and W. S. Fielding, who had deserted Laurier over the conscription crisis.[46] Diefenbaker's Cabinet was divided over many issues, including defence policy,[47] while Lester Pearson had difficulty in reconciling Walter Gordon's anti-American views with the business interests represented by Mitchell Sharp and Robert Winters.[48]

In the face of such Cabinet conflicts Prime Ministers have exhibited a variety of different styles of chairmanship. Lester Pearson often entered Cabinet meetings without a distinct point of view, and searched for a compromise between the extreme views expressed by his ministers.[49] He has observed of the difficult art of chairmanship:

> My style of conducting Cabinet meetings was relaxed, and informal; more so, I believe than was the case with my predecessors. Mackenzie King, you know, never allowed anyone to smoke in Cabinet or have a coffee or any other kind of break. He was the headmaster: Mr. St. Laurent's Cabinet was more formal than mine, but he was always a very considerate and courteous chairman, and anxious to encourage the widest participation in discussions.[50]

If King was the headmaster, R. B. Bennett was the autocrat.[51] He had no real experience of collective decision-making before becoming Prime Minister, as he had held office for only three months in 1921 and two months in 1926. As a lawyer and a businessman he had invariably worked alone, and he maintained this practice as Prime Minister. One comment on his Cabinet style is provided by a 1930s joke:

> Visitor to Ottawa: "Who is that man coming towards us?"
> Ottawa resident: "Mr. R. B. Bennett, the new Prime Minister."
> Visitor to Ottawa: "Why is he talking to himself?"
> Ottawa resident: "He is holding a Cabinet meeting."[52]

Sir Robert Borden was also capable of emphasizing the Prime Minister's authority. He records in his diary, for example, that at a Cabinet meeting on May 24th, 1917:

> The discussion [about the possible formation of a coalition
> government] was lengthy and eventually became so wearisome
> that I interposed, informing my colleagues that they had made
> me sufficiently acquainted with their views, that the duty of
> decision rested with me, and that I would subsequently make
> them acquainted with my conclusion.[53]

John Diefenbaker, in marked contrast, was frequently indecisive in Cabinet.[54] He carried the principle of collective
decision-making to its extreme, and was reluctant to recom-
mend any course of action that did not have unanimous
Cabinet approval. Wilfrid Laurier and Pierre Trudeau also
encouraged full Cabinet discussion: according to O. D. Skelton,
"In Cabinet Councils [Laurier] never played the dictator,"[55]
while Peter C. Newman claims that Trudeau "conducted
Cabinet meetings like a Jesuit seminar, allowing issues to be
fully aired, and bringing Ministers to his point of view, by
letting them talk."[56] Westell makes a similar point, describing
Trudeau's Cabinet style as being that of ". . . a consensus
leader who appointed energetic Ministers, encouraged them to
be innovative, and insisted on full discussion of alternatives
before decisions were made."[57]

Trudeau attempted to break the dominance of "the departmental point of view" in Cabinet discussions by asking ministers to present all the policy alternatives for any issue before
the Cabinet.[58] The development of the Cabinet committee
system under Pearson and Trudeau was also designed to some
extent to involve ministers in the consideration of policy
beyond their own departments. Eric Kierans, however, resigned
from the Cabinet in 1971 because he felt that ministers were
not sufficiently involved in general policy, and because he, in
particular, was not able to influence economic policy.[59]

b. Cabinet Relationships

Dawson and Ward argue that:

> A Prime Minister who would try to issue orders to his Ministers
> or would interfere persistently in their departmental work might
> find that before long he was out of office; for if at any time

the ministers chose to rebel, their combined influence in the party and in the House could, and in all likelihood would, bring about his speedy downfall.[60]

The triangular relationship between the Prime Minister, a departmental minister, and the rest of the Cabinet is a complex one, however, in which the "balance of influence" will vary from situation to situation. Just what are the possible variations in the relationship? Five main "permutations" can be identified:

Situation A: Prime Minister *plus* the rest of the Cabinet *versus* the departmental minister.

        B: Prime Minister *plus* one section of the Cabinet *versus* the department minister *plus* another section of the Cabinet.

        C: Prime Minister *versus* the departmental minister *plus* the rest of the Cabinet.

        D: Prime Minister *plus* the departmental minister *versus* the rest of the Cabinet.

        E: Prime Minister *plus* the departmental minister *plus* one section of the Cabinet *versus* another section of the Cabinet.

When the Prime Minister can unite most or all of the Cabinet behind him in opposition to a departmental minister's stand (Situation A), the Prime Minister's chances of imposing his view normally will be great. Thus in 1903 Laurier used Cabinet consensus to overcome the objections of A. G. Blair, the Minister of Railways, towards the second trans-continental railway (and Blair subsequently resigned over the issue).[61] Mackenzie King, in 1928, secured Cabinet support for tariff cuts, against the better judgment of the Tariff Board and the Revenue Minister.[62] In March 1967 Lester Pearson and the Cabinet persuaded Mitchell Sharp, then Finance Minister, not to amend the Bank Act in order to give concessions to American banks in Canada.[63]

Nevertheless, while few departmental ministers will be powerful enough to survive a confrontation with the Prime Minister and a united Cabinet, a minister may be astute enough to present issues to Cabinet in such a way as to retain the real initiative in his own hands. Paul Martin's handling of foreign policy in Pearson's government perhaps illustrates this. Martin was adept at presenting foreign policy matters in technical terms that baffled the Cabinet. Pearson himself was prepared to leave most matters in Martin's hands, but on the occasions when he did try to influence an issue, Martin's skill and knowledge were such that "by coming up with some new proposal for procedural review, [Martin] would be able to resist the pressure for what he regarded as popular concessions."[64] He resisted and delayed, for example, Pearson's call for a major review of foreign policy in the 1965-68 Parliament, and when eventually it could be delayed no longer, Martin was able to ensure that it was undertaken by someone sympathetic to the department's work.[65]

When the rest of the Cabinet is itself divided on an issue on which the Prime Minister and departmental minister are in conflict (Situation B), the Prime Minister's chances of success are uncertain. Much will depend on the number and status of the ministers who choose to oppose the Prime Minister, and on the flexibility of the individuals concerned. Bowell's resignation in 1896 followed from such a divided Cabinet situation. On the other hand, Trudeau in 1969 successfully overcame Cabinet opposition to his views on Canada's NATO role.[66] Indeed, the Trudeau policy (that Canada should remain a member of NATO, but with fewer troops in Europe) was adopted despite the opposition of the two departmental ministers most directly involved, the majority of senior officials, the House of Commons Committee on External Affairs, and a large part of the Liberal caucus. Of this episode Bruce Thordarson concluded that:

> [Trudeau] was prepared to give and take on minor tactical questions, but . . . it was his influence that determined that basic philosophy on which the [final] decision was based.[67]

Mackenzie King's premiership provides many similar examples of the exercise of prime-ministerial initiative in the face of Cabinet opposition. Despite strong objections voiced at a particularly stormy Cabinet meeting in December 1924, King insisted that the government pursue a policy of making concessions to the Prairie provinces in an attempt to undermine the western appeal of the Progressive Party.[68] Again, after the 1925 election, when his government lost its overall majority, King refused to bow to Cabinet demands for a re-allocation of ministerial posts, insisting that this was essentially his prerogative.[69] In his last year or so as Prime Minister, King became increasingly suspicious of his Cabinet, and reserved more and more decisions to himself.[70] No Prime Minister, however, can afford to become completely isolated within his Cabinet (Situation C) on a succession of issues. A Prime Minister who sees such a division emerging normally will avoid a confrontation by giving way, or, when it is possible, postponing the issue to allow time for the ministerial alliances to be undermined (as King frequently did).

Situations A, B, and C involve conflict on an item of departmental policy between the Prime Minister and the minister most directly concerned. On many issues, however, the Prime Minister and the departmental minister will be in agreement. Here, a powerful temporary alliance can be formed to persuade the rest of the Cabinet to accept "the departmental point of view" (Situation D). Finance and foreign affairs are two key areas in which the Prime Minister will frequently seek to work closely with the departmental minister, to the exclusion of other ministers. Sir Robert Borden and W. T. White, his Finance Minister, often decided tariff policy themselves in order to "avoid protracted discussion in Council".[71] Today, the preparation of budget proposals is the exclusive concern of the Finance Minister in consultation with the Prime Minister.[72] Other ministers are not usually informed of the budget details until a Cabinet meeting on the day of its presentation to the House. Throughout Lester Pearson's premiership there was very little Cabinet discussion of foreign policy, as Pearson and the External Affairs Minister, Paul Martin, would settle most matters themselves. The policy of unifying the armed forces was discussed only twice in Cabinet, and in the last year of the Pearson government the only foreign policy matter that was dealt with at all seriously in Cabinet was the renewal of the NORAD agreement.[73]

The virtual exclusion of Trudeau and other ministers from any consideration of foreign policy under Pearson was one reason why Martin was not reappointed External Affairs Minister when Trudeau became Prime Minister,[74] and why there was a demand in 1968 for open Cabinet discussion of Canada's NATO role. In practice, however, Mitchell Sharp, as External Affairs Minister under Trudeau, continued to enjoy a considerable degree of freedom of action, and with the exception of the NATO decision and a few other matters, the Cabinet has not concerned itself greatly with foreign affairs.[75] There is no great tradition in Canada, of course, of Cabinet involvement in foreign policy. In the nineteenth century it was essentially an Imperial matter, with the Prime Minister dealing personally with the British government, while in the modern world it has been increasingly a matter for summit meetings of foreign ministers and heads of government. More than this, however, few individual Cabinet ministers will be sufficiently politically powerful to challenge an alliance between the Prime Minister and the External Affairs Minister, while, in any case, most ministers are primarily concerned with regional and other domestic matters.

The chances of success for a minister-Prime Minister alliance are particularly good when the rest of the Cabinet is divided on the issue (Situation E). Even so, success for the alliance is not guaranteed. The contents of Walter Gordon's controversial first budget in 1963 were not revealed to the Cabinet until Budget Day itself, and Pearson was opposed even to Cabinet committee discussion of the proposal in case this led to changes being made.[76] After the budget's introduction, however, Gordon was obliged to make amendments because of criticism of some of the proposals by other ministers. Gordon claimed that on this occasion Pearson was slow to support him in face of these Cabinet criticisms.[77]

HOLDING THE TEAM TOGETHER

a. The Prime Minister as Executioner

The ultimate weapon available to the Prime Minister in any Cabinet dispute is the dismissal of one or more of his ministers.

The Prime Minister appoints and thus can dismiss — although it may not always be practical for him to do so. As noted earlier,[78] there may be no adequate replacement, while even if there is a possible successor, a dismissal reflects badly upon the Prime Minister's ability to select wisely, causes bad publicity, and can create a martyr. The offending minister may well have support in the Cabinet or in Parliament or among the electorate. Because of the big electoral following for Sir Sam Hughes, the troublesome Minister of Militia and Defence in the First World War, it was two years before Borden responded to the Cabinet rumblings against him.[79]

Ultimately, however, incompetent, difficult, and embarassing ministers may have to be dismissed, and here the Prime Minister has to be an efficient executioner. Laurier was reputedly a firm Prime Minister in this respect, dismissing Israel Tarte for publicly opposing the government's commitment to a policy of reduced tariffs. Laurier's letter of dismissal to Tarte remains as a classic statement of a minister's obligations under collective responsibility:

> If you had not been able to obtain from your colleagues their assent to the course which you recommended, you would have been obliged then either to accept their own views or to sever your connection with them, and then for the first time would you have been free to place your views before the public.[80]

Trudeau demonstrated his strength in this regard after the 1974 election, when five ministers were removed from the government.

The Prime Minister, of course, can attempt to remove a minister by more subtle means than a public dismissal. A minister who has ceased to be an asset can be elevated to the Senate, as were Alfred Brooks and Henry Courtmanche in 1960, or persuaded to accept a post outside Parliament, as when the controversial Joseph Cauchon was made Lieutenant-Governor of Quebec in 1960.

Again, a minister who has become a liability in a particular department, but who can still make a contribution to the government, can be moved horizontally to another post. In 1964 Guy Favreau felt that he should resign because of his involvement in the Rivard scandal, but he was persuaded to remain in the Cabinet in another post.[81] A minister may not always agree to be "reshuffled" in this way, however. Diefenbaker had difficulty in 1962 in persuading Donald Fleming to move to the Ministry of Justice from Finance after the Coyne affair,[82] while Walter Gordon twice refused to move from Finance when Pearson suggested it after the controversial budgets of 1963 and 1964.[83]

Even more subtly, the Prime Minister, or the minister's enemies, can manipulate a situation in which the minister has little option but to resign. Paul Hellyer, for example, found himself in 1969 in a position where he had either to resign or lose a considerable amount of face when the Cabinet would not support the housing and urban-planning policies that he had publicly championed. The politics of ministerial resignations, however, are complex. Just what factors do govern this aspect of the Cabinet system?

b. Ministerial Resignations

Resignations (as opposed to "retirements" for health or similar reasons) can be provoked by a variety of factors. A minister may be in disagreement with his colleagues over policy, either because the Cabinet has rejected a policy to which he or his department was strongly committed (as when Sir William Mulock resigned in 1905 over the government's rejection of the policy of a publicly owned telephone system)[84] or because he cannot accept policies that have emerged from other departments (as with Eric Kierans' resignation in 1971 over broad economic policy).[85] Such a resignation may be a dramatic public gesture to draw attention to an issue — a form of ministerial pyrotechnics. Alternatively the minister may develop an aversion to one of his Cabinet colleagues, or to the Prime Minister himself, either for personality reasons or because of the regional or group interest they represent (as with Sir Francis Hincks' resignation in 1873 over the anti-Imperial sentiments expressed by Joseph Howe).[86] Again, the minister may resign because he has become generally disenchanted with federal politics (as with Walter Gordon's resignation in 1968).[87]

Resignations can cause major problems for the Prime Minister. The series of resignations from Bowell's Cabinet in 1895 and 1896 led eventually to Bowell's own resignation.[88] No other Prime Minister has faced quite so dramatic and damaging a revolt, but a number have had their difficulties. Macdonald was troubled by a series of resignations and threatened resignations early in the life of his first Cabinet, and at one stage the government's viability was in doubt.[89] He had particular difficulty keeping a Minister of Finance — with Sir Alexander Galt, Sir John Rose, and Sir Francis Hincks resigning from the post in turn. Clifford Sifton resigned from Laurier's Cabinet in February 1905 over the Alberta schools issue, despite Laurier's confidence that a compromise could be worked out between the "Protestant" and "Catholic" wings of the Cabinet.[90] The loss of this key Prairie figure almost led to the government's downfall, as a number of MPs supported Sifton's stand. Major divisions appeared in Diefenbaker's Cabinet in its last few months, and there was a series of resignations.[91] Douglas Harkness, the Defence Minister, resigned in January 1963 over Diefenbaker's attitude to the acquisition of nuclear warheads, and George Hees and others led a Cabinet revolt over this. Subsequently, Hees and Pierre Sévigny resigned at the beginning of the election campaign in 1963, and Davie Fulton, Donald Fleming, and Ernest Halpenny resigned during the campaign for what they claimed were "personal reasons".

The Prime Minister may find himself faced with threats of resignation from two sides in a Cabinet conflict. This was Bowell's problem in the Cabinet crises over the Manitoba schools issue in 1895-96, and this danger is inherent in any issue that touches on the basic regional, religious, or ethnic divisions of Canada. During the Second World War, for example, Mackenzie King had to contend with threats of resignations, and then actual resignations, from both pro- and anti-conscriptionists in the Cabinet. In May 1942 Pierre Cardin resigned when it seemed as though King was moving towards the introduction of conscription, and C. G. Power resigned in November 1944 when eventually it was introduced.[92] The feeling among the pro-conscriptionists, however, was that King was paying too much attention to the susceptibilities of the

Quebec ministers, and eventually James Ralston resigned because of this.[93]

The impact made by ministerial resignations will be dependent upon a variety of factors — the minister, the issue, the timing, public feeling on the issue, and the manner in which it is handled by the Prime Minister. Most resignations cause little more than a momentary flurry, and Cabinet history is littered with examples of largely inconsequential resignations. Borden, for example, easily survived the resignations of Louis Peletier and Wilfrid Nantel in 1914, and Albert Sévigny in 1918, over war policy,[94] while Bennett was largely untroubled by the resignation of H. H. Stevens in 1934.[95] Walter Gordon's resignation in February 1968 made little impact, as it came when the press were concentrating on the party-leadership race that was then in progress. Similarly, the resignations of Paul Hellyer in 1969 and Eric Kierans in 1971 caused no more than "a little local difficulty" for Trudeau.

The *threat* of resignation can be used as a weapon in Cabinet battles, but the threat may never be carried out for one reason or another. The Prime Minister, for example, may be able to persuade the minister to back down. Macdonald persuaded John Costigan not to resign over the financing of the CPR in 1885,[96] while Pearson prevailed upon Walter Gordon not to resign over criticisms of his 1963 budget.[97] The threat of resignation may be enough to persuade the Prime Minister and the Cabinet to accept the minister's point of view. King was opposed to Canada being appointed to a United Nations Commission on Korea, but he gave way to St. Laurent's wishes on this.[98] King regarded C. D. Howe as being indispensable, and gave way to him when he threatened to resign over the handling of a war-time labour dispute.[99] Paul Hellyer's threats to resign in 1966 persuaded Pearson and the Cabinet to persevere with the scheme for integrating the armed forces, despite the cries of anguish from the military.[100] Similarly, in the face of a threat of resignation by Bryce Mackasey in 1969, the Trudeau Cabinet agreed to support his new unemployment insurance scheme,[101] while in 1974 the Cabinet gave way when James Richardson, the Defence Minister and MP for Winnipeg South, threatened not to seek re-election unless the government restored Air Canada's repair facilities to Winnipeg.[102] Alternatively, the minister may back down in the face of a firm stand by the Prime Minister. In April 1916 the Quebec ministers T. C. Casgrain, Pierre Blondin, and Leon Patenaude threatened to resign if Borden did not intervene to protect French-language rights in Ontario, but they eventually gave way when Borden refused to take action.[103]

The Prime Minister himself may threaten to resign in order to persuade the Cabinet, or an individual minister, to accept his point of view. Most Prime Ministers will use this tactic at one time or another. Borden offered to resign in face of the difficulties he encountered in forming the coalition government in 1917, but as there was no real alternative Prime Minister available there was no likelihood of his resignation being accepted.[104] King also often threatened to resign, knowing that his ability to win general elections made him indispensable to the party. In 1944 he threatened to resign in the face of the pressures exerted on him by pro-conscriptionist ministers,[105] but eventually he had to accede to their wishes. St. Laurent used the threat of resignation to persuade the Cabinet to support C. D. Howe's parliamentary tactics over the Trans-Canada Pipe Line issue in 1956,[106] while Diefenbaker threatened to resign in February 1963 in an effort (partially successful) to silence Cabinet criticism of him over defence policy.[107] Pearson threatened to resign unless the Cabinet approved a list of dubious "political" appointments to the Senate.[108]

c. A Fluctuating Membership

In addition to dismissals and resignations that result from policy or other conflicts within the Cabinet, ministers may leave the Cabinet as a result of a variety of "accidental" factors. Ministers may be forced to retire, for example, through ill-health. Joe Green left Trudeau's Cabinet in 1972 after a heart attack, while Jean-Paul Deschatelets retired from Pearson's Cabinet in 1965 following a family tragedy. Again, ministers will be obliged to resign if they lose their parliamentary seats, as did Harry Hays and J. W. McNaught at the 1965 election and Jack Davis at the 1974 election. Others may voluntarily leave

Parliament in order to take up posts outside. Six members of the Cabinet that Laurier formed in 1896 soon left to take up provincial or judicial appointments. Jack Pickersgill left Pearson's Cabinet to become head of the Canadian Transport Commission in 1967, and Leo Cadieux left Trudeau's Cabinet in 1970 to become Ambassador to France. Robert Winters resigned from Pearson's Cabinet in March 1968 so that he could devote all of his time to the party-leadership campaign then in progress, while Walter Gordon resigned as a "debt of honour" when the 1965 dissolution of Parliament, which he had strongly urged, failed to yield the government the overall parliamentary majority it sought. Such retirements can combine with policy resignations and dismissals to produce major changes in the Cabinet in a comparatively short time. A third of Macdonald's carefully constructed 1867 Cabinet left within the first twelve months. Of the fourteen ministers appointed by Mackenzie in 1873, only four survived until 1878, with only three retaining the same post throughout. Lester Pearson lost the services of five ministers during 1965 (Dupuis, Deschatelets, Gordon, Lamontagne, and Tremblay) and lost another five in the last twelve months of the government's life (Cardin, Favreau, Pickersgill, Winters, and Gordon again). Such a rapid turnover, of course, can help a new Prime Minister to establish his personal ascendency within the Cabinet. When Laurier became Prime Minister in 1896 he was surrounded by a number of powerful and experienced ministers, but by the end of his government's life all of his ministers had entered Parliament after 1896 and owed their advancement to him. J. W. Dafoe commented on this that:

> It is in keeping with the genius of our party system that the leader who begins as the chosen chief of his associates proceeds by stages . . . to a position of dominance; the republic is transformed into an absolute monarchy.[109]

A similar pattern can be found in Trudeau's Cabinet, as shown in Table 5:1. Three-quarters of the Cabinet he formed in April 1968 were inherited from Pearson, and all but one of these had more ministerial experience than Trudeau had. As a result of changes made after the 1969 election, however, the Cabinet was fairly evenly balanced between ex-Pearson ministers and new recruits, while after the 1972 election two-thirds of the Cabinet had been recruited by Trudeau.

Table 5:1

TRUDEAU CABINET — 1968-74

	Total (excluding PM)	Recruited by Trudeau	Previous Cabinet Experience
April 1968	24	6	18
July 1968	28	13	15
Sept. 1970	28	15	13
Jan. 1972	28	17	11
Nov. 1972	29	22	7
July 1974	28	22	6

SOURCE: J. K. Johnson, ed., *The Canadian Directory of Parliament* (Ottawa: Public Archives of Canada, 1968) (up-dated from Keesing's Archives).

At the same time, the loss of a number of ministers, or of just one or two key ministers, can weaken the credibility and authority of the Cabinet and the Prime Minister. At the very least it deprives the Cabinet of men of talent and influence, and can make difficult the acquisition of Cabinet team spirit and self-knowledge. It may divide the party at all levels and can create centres of discontent outside the Cabinet. Thus in 1872 John A. Macdonald argued strongly against the dismissal of Joseph Howe from the Cabinet, despite his embarrassing anti-British speeches, lest he "rekindle the expiring flame of discontent in the Maritimes".[110] Upheavals that occur close to an election can damage the party's prospects of retaining office, and the series of resignations from Diefenbaker's Cabinet in 1963 almost certainly contributed to its electoral defeat. At the very least, the search for replacements can be difficult and time-consuming. Even a limited reshuffling of posts can cause great difficulties, as is well illustrated by a succinct entry in Sir Robert Borden's diary:

> *Tuesday, November 5* [1918]. Excursions and alarms all day respecting reconstruction of Government. Telegram from Pardee that he cannot come in. Conference with Rowell and afterwards with Calder, Carvell, Rowell and Reid as to Nesbitt, Lloyd

Harris and Cronyn. Liberals could not agree. Sent for Ballan-
tyne and pressed him to accept Trade and Commerce. He was
unwilling and I gave it up . . .[111]

Emphasis on ministerial resignations and dismissals, however, should not be allowed to obscure the fact that the majority of ministers are not involved in such dramatic confrontations with Prime Ministers. Most ministers remain under the
umbrella of collective responsibility, and give up their posts
only when their party leaves office, or when they retire for
non-political reasons such as ill-health and old age, or when
they are overlooked by the Prime Minister in a ministerial
reshuffle. Even separatists like Howe of Nova Scotia in the
1870s, and Don Jamieson of Newfoundland in the 1970s,
became converted into "Federal Canadians" through membership in the Cabinet. Among the considerations that will deter
resignation are personal loyalty to the Prime Minister or other
ministers, loyalty to the party and the desire to avoid damaging
it, the desire for promotion within the ministerial hierarchy, the
relative obscurity that may well follow departure from the
federal scene, and the "protection" that is provided by the
principles of Cabinet secrecy and collective responsibility. More
than any of these considerations, however, membership in the
federal Cabinet provides major tangible rewards in the form
of the ability to influence national affairs, pursue policy initiatives, and obtain benefits for a region, or ethnic or religious
group. The extent to which a minister is able to obtain these
rewards, however, will depend ultimately on the manner in
which the Cabinet's decision-making process operates.

CONCLUSIONS

While the Cabinet may be too unwieldy to work effectively as
a day-to-day decision-making body, it remains sufficiently
powerful to undermine any notions that the Canadian system
is characterized by the prime-ministerial or ministerial decision-
making models. Thus of the four models that were outlined at
the beginning of this chapter, we are left with the inner-group
model. Patrick Gordon Walker, himself a former British
Cabinet minister, has argued that the British system is now

characterized, not by prime-ministerial government, as so many people have claimed, but by government by an inner-group of the Cabinet. He calls this inner group a "partial Cabinet":

> I use this term to denote a number of Ministers who constitute part only of the Cabinet but act for a time as if they were the Cabinet. . . . A partial Cabinet is the very opposite of Prime Ministerial government: it presupposes that the Prime Minister carries influential Cabinet colleagues with him, and that these will, with the Prime Minister, convince the Cabinet if policy is questioned when the Cabinet is informed.[112]

Can this interpretation of the manner in which the British Cabinet system operates be applied equally well to Canadian government? When talking of an inner group of the Cabinet a distinction has to be drawn between, on the one hand, a formal Inner Cabinet or senior Cabinet committee with a regular routine of meetings and a fixed membership, and on the other, an informal inner group with no fixed routines and perhaps a fluctuating membership. In most Cabinets there will be an informal inner core of particularly able and influential members upon whom the Prime Minister will particularly rely. Macdonald, Cartier, Galt, and Tilley formed a natural inner group in Macdonald's first Cabinet,[113] while Laurier's Cabinet in 1896 had a natural inner group of Fielding, Mowat, Tarte, Mulock, Sifton, and Cartwright, with the other ten ministers being of limited ability and influence.[114]

As well as such informal cliques, based largely on personal relationships with the Prime Minister, have Canadian Cabinets contained more formal inner groups? To some extent a "functional Inner Cabinet" exists in every Cabinet, made up of the holders of the five traditional co-ordinative posts — External Affairs, Finance, Justice, Treasury Board, and the Prime Minister himself. Again, under Trudeau the Priorities and Planning Committee is very close to being an Inner Cabinet in the sense that it contains the principal ministers, meets more often than the Cabinet as a whole, and is the real decision-making body on some key issues.[115] Such a purely functional grouping, however, inevitably will be refined by factors like personal loyalty to the Prime Minister, and influence based on regional or group support.

On various occasions during Lester Pearson's premiership, Walter Gordon pressed for the introduction of a formal Inner Cabinet.[116] He felt that Pearson was out of touch with his ministers, and relied too much upon the advice of Tom Kent and one or two other personal friends. Gordon hoped that Pearson's Cabinet committee system would produce an "inner council" of the seven committee chairmen, plus Pearson. When this did not happen, Gordon pressed Pearson in June 1964 to introduce a system of six to eight senior ministers meeting daily. Pearson did not take any action, and Gordon revived the proposal in 1967, suggesting a daily meeting of a six-man "Policy Committee" and a weekly meeting of the full Cabinet. Again, however, while Pearson agreed that it was a desirable reform, he took no action.

To some extent Pearson's caution on this matter was because of the fundamental problem, inherent in the whole concept of an Inner Cabinet, of how to satisfy all regions and groups that their interests will be defended in a small decision-making body in which they may not be represented. Thus G. B. Doern has pointed out:

> It is probably safe to predict that such a full-blown inner and outer Cabinet system will never occur in Canada, given the strength and importance of regional and ethnic representation in the Cabinet . . . .[117]

This objection, however, does not apply to quite the same extent to the concept of an informal inner group, with a membership that fluctuates somewhat according to the issue under consideration. Of all the decision-making models that have been looked at in this chapter, then, it is this concept of an informal, "floating" inner group (or, to adapt Gordon Walker, an "informal partial Cabinet") that seems to come closest to the realities of the decision-making process in the Canadian Cabinet system.

NOTES

1. Ernest Watkins, *R. B. Bennett: A Biography* (London: Secker and Warburg, 1963), p. 170.
2. R. M. Dawson and N. Ward, *The Government of Canada* (Toronto: University of Toronto Press, 1963), p. 207.

3. W. Buckingham and G. W. Ross, *The Hon. Alexander Mackenzie* (New York: Greenwood Press, 1969), p. 442.
4. O. D. Skelton, *Life and Letters of Sir Wilfrid Laurier* (London: Oxford University Press, 1922), II: 163.
5. P. C. Newman, *The Distemper of Our Times* (Toronto: McClelland and Stewart, 1968), pp. 52, 197.
6. B. Thordarson, *Trudeau and Foreign Policy* (Toronto: Oxford University Press, 1972), p. 155.
7. Newman, *The Distemper of Our Times* p. 255.
8. Judy LaMarsh, *Memoirs of a Bird in a Gilded Cage* (Toronto: McClelland and Stewart, 1969), p. 93.
9. Ibid., pp. 63, 260.
10. D. Smith, *Gentle Patriot: A Political Biography of Walter Gordon* (Edmonton: Hurtig, 1973), p. 256; LaMarsh, *Memoirs*, p. 328.
11. T. A. Hockin, ed., *Apex of Power* (Toronto: Prentice-Hall, 1971), p. 258.
12. P. C. Dobell, *Canada's Search for New Roles: Foreign Policy in the Trudeau Era* (London: Oxford University Press, 1972), pp. 14-15.
13. A. Westell, *Paradox: Trudeau as Prime Minister* (Toronto: Prentice-Hall, 1972), p. 231.
14. For a comment see D. Creighton, *John A. Macdonald* (Toronto: Macmillan, 1955-56), II: 523.
15. R. B. Farrell, *The Making of Canadian Foreign Policy* (Toronto: Prentice-Hall, 1969), pp. 37-40.
16. Hockin, *Apex of Power*, p. 206.
17. Farrell, *The Making of Canadian Foreign Policy*, p. 11.
18. Ibid., p. 12.
19. Ibid., p. 12.
20. G. B. Doern and P. Aucoin, *The Structures of Policy Making in Canada* (Toronto: Macmillan, 1971), p. 46.
21. P. C. Newman, *Renegade in Power* (Toronto: McClelland and Stewart, 1964), p. 347.
22. H. B. Neatby, *William Lyon Mackenzie King, 1924-32* (Toronto: University of Toronto Press, 1963), p. 360.
23. Skelton, *Life and Letters of Sir Wilfrid Laurier*, pp. 6-13.
24. See above p. 58.
25. R. M. Dawson's phrase in Dawson and Ward, *The Government of Canada*, p. 171.
26. See Judy LaMarsh's descriptions of meetings of the Pearson Cabinet in her *Memoirs*, pp. 51-2.
27. Creighton, *John A. Macdonald*, II: 312.
28. Smith, *Gentle Patriot*, p. 169; LaMarsh, *Memoirs*, p. 65.
29. Newman, *Renegade in Power*, p. 93.
30. Creighton, *John A. Macdonald*, II: 11.

31. A. D. P. Heeney, "Cabinet Government in Canada", *Canadian Journal of Economics and Political Science*, 1946, pp. 282-301.
32. LaMarsh, *Memoirs*, p. 141.
33. Hockin, *Apex of Power*, p. 259.
34. Walter Stewart, *Shrug: Trudeau in Power* (Toronto: New Press, 1972), p. 162.
35. Dobell, *Canada's Search for New Roles*, p. 14.
36. Smith, *Gentle Patriot*, p. 140.
37. LaMarsh, *Memoirs*, p. 160.
38. Skelton, *Life and Letters of Sir Wilfrid Laurier*, II: 97.
39. H. Borden, ed., *Robert Laird Borden: His Memoirs* (London: Macmillan, 1938), p. 455.
40. Dawson and Ward, *The Government of Canada*, p. 249.
41. Ibid., p. 249.
42. Arnold Heeney, *The Things That are Caesar's* (Toronto: University of Toronto Press, 1972), p. 76.
43. See above p. 107.
44. J. Schull, *Laurier: The First Canadian* (Toronto: Macmillan, 1965), p. 340.
45. Ibid., p. 414.
46. Neatby, *William Lyon Mackenzie King: 1924-32*, p. 5.
47. Newman, *Renegade in Power*, p. 95.
48. See, for example, Smith, *Gentle Patriot*, p. 169.
49. Newman, *The Distemper of Our Times*, p. 210.
50. Hockin, *Apex of Power*, p. 197.
51. Watkins, *R. B. Bennett: A Biography*, p. 167.
52. Ibid., p. 167.
53. Borden, *Robert Laird Borden: His Memoirs*, p. 720.
54. For contrasting views of Diefenbaker's performance in Cabinet, see P. Stursburg, *Leadership Gained 1956-62* (Toronto: University of Toronto Press, 1975), and Newman, *Renegade in Power*.
55. Skelton, *Life and Letters of Sir Wilfrid Laurier*, II: 163.
56. Newman, *Maclean's*, January 1973, p. 64.
57. Westell, *Paradox: Trudeau as Prime Minister*, p. 232.
58. Thordarson, *Trudeau and Foreign Policy*, p. 92.
59. W. Stewart, "Baby, It Was Cold Inside: Eric Kierans Reveals How Trudeau Froze Him Out", *Maclean's*, July 1971, p. 64.
60. Dawson and Ward, *The Government of Canada*, p. 203.
61. Skelton, *Life and Letters of Sir Wilfrid Laurier*, II: 189.
62. Neatby, *William Lyon Mackenzie King*, p. 246.
63. Smith, *Gentle Patriot*, p. 319.
64. Dobell, *Canada's Search for New Roles*, p. 12.
65. Thordarson, *Trudeau and Foreign Policy*, p. 26.
66. Ibid., p. 159.

67. Ibid., p. 162.
68. Neatby, *William Lyon Mackenzie King*, p. 29.
69. Ibid., p. 86.
70. Bruce Hutchison, *Mr. Prime Minister: 1867-1964* (Don Mills: Longmans, 1964), p. 282.
71. Borden, *Robert Laird Borden: His Memoirs*, p. 392.
72. W. Stewart, "Baby, It Was Cold Inside: Eric Kierans Reveals How Trudeau Froze Him Out", *Maclean's*, July 1971, p. 64.
73. Dobell, *Canada's Search for New Roles*, p. 11.
74. Ibid., p. 13.
75. Farrell, *The Making of Canadian Foreign Policy*, p. 13.
76. Smith, *Gentle Patriot*, p. 150.
77. Ibid., pp. 169, 178.
78. See p. 67.
79. Skelton, *Life and Letters of Sir Wilfrid Laurier*, II: 429.
80. Skelton, *Life and Letters of Sir Wilfrid Laurier*, I: 181.
81. Smith, *Gentle Patriot*, p. 240.
82. Hutchison, *Mr. Prime Minister*, p. 335.
83. Smith, *Gentle Patriot*, pp. 212, 252.
84. Borden, *Robert Laird Borden: His Memoirs*, I: 140.
85. Stewart, *Maclean's*, July 1971, p. 32.
86. Sir Joseph Pope, ed., *Memoirs of Sir John A. Macdonald*, (London: Arnold, 1894), II: 154.
87. Smith, *Gentle Patriot*, pp. 346-7.
88. For details see below p. 143.
89. Pope, *Memoirs of Sir John A. Macdonald*, II: 4, 70, and 154.
90. Skelton, *Life and Letters of Sir Wilfrid Laurier*, II: 230.
91. Newman, *Renegade in Power*, pp. 364-98.
92. Farrell, *The Making of Canadian Foreign Policy*, p. 14.
93. Ibid., p. 14.
94. Borden, *Robert Laird Borden: His Memoirs*, II: 471, 475.
95. Watkins, *R. B. Bennett*, p. 208.
96. Sir Joseph Pope, ed., *Correspondence of Sir John A. Macdonald* (Toronto: Oxford University Press, 1921), p. 330.
97. Smith, *Gentle Patriot*, p. 165.
98. Hutchison, *Mr. Prime Minister*, p. 291.
99. Ibid., p. 302.
100. LaMarsh, *Memoirs*, p. 315.
101. Westell, *Paradox: Trudeau as Prime Minister*, p. 171.
102. Marci McDonald, "Always the Young Stranger", *Maclean's*, March 1975, p. 47.
103. Borden, *Robert Laird Borden: His Memoirs*, II: 575.
104. Ibid., pp. 747, 797.
105. Hutchison, *Mr. Prime Minister*, p. 269.
106. Newman, *Renegade in Power*, p. 143.
107. Ibid., p. 363.

108. LaMarsh *Memoirs,* p. 291.
109. J. W. Dafoe, *Laurier: A Study in Canadian Politics* (Toronto: Allen, 1922), p. 131.
110. Pope, *Correspondence of Sir John A. Macdonald,* p. 161.
111. Borden, *Robert Laird Borden: His Memoirs,* II: 862.
112. P. Gordon Walker, *The Cabinet* (London: Cape, 1970), pp. 88, 91.
113. Hutchinson, *Mr. Prime Minister,* p. 18.
114. Ibid., p. 120.
115. R. J. Van Loon and M. S. Whittington, *The Canadian Political System* (Toronto: McGraw-Hill, 1971), p. 382.
116. Smith, *Gentle Patriot,* pp. 196, 201, 331.
117. Doern and Aucoin, *The Structures of Policy Making in Canada,* p. 74.

6. The Fusion of Powers

"He who doesn't know Parliament cannot be a good Prime Minister."[1] Thus John Diefenbaker has pointed to the importance of the parliamentary aspects of a Prime Minister's role. But precisely what is the nature of the Prime Minister's involvement with Parliament? Four main aspects can be identified. In the first place, the Prime Minister is a member of Parliament. Constitutional convention requires that he must have a seat in one of the Houses of Parliament, and modern circumstances demand that this be in the Commons rather than in the Senate. He is not selected by members of Parliament, however, and although as Prime Minister he has to be skilled in parliamentary techniques, he does not necessarily have to demonstrate these skills before acquiring the job.

Second, the Prime Minister organizes the business of Parliament. In consultation with his Cabinet, and in particular with the minister who bears the title of House Leader, the Prime Minister determines when Parliament will meet, the length of its sessions, the nature of much of its business, and the distribution of parliamentary time among the various items of business. His control is not absolute, of course, in that there are certain constitutional ground rules regarding the summoning of Parliament and the nature of its procedures that cannot be ignored. Within such basic limitations, however, the Prime Minister exercises considerable control over parliamentary affairs. Thus Trudeau, despite much criticism, was able to delay the summoning of Parliament, and the announcement of his legislative plans, for ten weeks after his victory in the 1974 general election.

Third, the Prime Minister attends and participates in the

Commons' deliberations. He votes in divisions, answers questions, speaks in debates, and supports the passage of legislation. He is essentially the government's field-commander in the House. Just how much time he spends in the field, and the priority he gives to Parliament as opposed to his other duties, will depend on a number of variables. The nature of the business before the House, the size of the government's majority, the competence of his lieutenants and of the Opposition, and his own inclinations, will all be important in this. The Prime Minister is obliged to attend at certain times, however, to answer questions and take part in major debates. Certainly, when Parliament is dealing with items of prime political or constitutional significance the Prime Minister is almost always the chief spokesman for the government.

Fourth, it is the Prime Minister who advises the Governor General when a dissolution of Parliament should take place and the public be asked to elect a new Parliament. The Prime Minister's decision has to be made within the five year maximum life of a Parliament. He is also restricted by the several practical considerations that affect the choice of an election date (and these are examined in detail in the next chapter). Nevertheless, the Prime Minister wields the ultimate power of life or death over a Parliament.

In these four vital respects the Prime Minister's role is intertwined with that of Parliament. Taken together they indicate the extent to which the Canadian Constitution is based upon the theory of the *fusion* of powers, as opposed to that of the *separation* of powers which underlies the American Constitution. The basic constitutional principles involved are that a Prime Minister and his ministers must report their activities to Parliament, and must retain the confidence of the majority of the members of the Commons, with a defeat on a major issue being an indication that this confidence has been lost. Although it is arguable just what constitutes a "major" issue, some matters, such as formal motions of no confidence, clearly are of prime significance. In face of a defeat on such an issue, a government is obliged either to resign, or to seek a dissolution of Parliament and present the issue to the electorate.

This represents the classic theory of government-Parliament relations. It is fashionable now, however, to revise the theory by underplaying the significance of a government's answerability and responsibility to Parliament. According to this "revisionist" view, the parliamentary procedures of question time, debates, and select committee enquiry are ineffective means of probing executive actions. In debates and at question time (it is argued) the Prime Minister and his ministers can be evasive, or can simply decline to give information, while even if they are "grilled" in the House the public impact will be only marginal. Further, according to the revisionist view, the government's vulnerability to a defeat in Parliament is not great: the strength of discipline within caucus and the extent of the government's control over the parliamentary timetable (particularly its power to overcome obstruction and speed the passage of legislation) turn a seemingly vulnerable government position into one of great strength. The revisionist view thus sees the Prime Minister as being in a more advantageous position than an American president. The Prime Minister is virtually as secure as a president between elections, and has the distinct advantage over the president of enjoying a secure majority for his policies in Parliament. The revisionist case has perhaps been put most succinctly by Professor Denis Smith, with his claim that "We seem to have created in Canada a presidential system without its congressional advantages."[2]

The revisionist view itself, however, needs to be qualified, as it minimizes the importance of two factors. It underestimates the extent to which parliamentary appearances can be a real ordeal for at least some Prime Ministers and ministers, and, more importantly, it underestimates the extent to which a Prime Minister's security of tenure, and the security of his policies, are achieved only through the preservation of a delicate balance of power between the Prime Minister and his backbenchers. What is more, when an election produces a minority government this balance of power has to be extended to encompass the minor parties. To this extent the presidential comparisons that are contained in the revisionist theory are misleading.

Just how far is the Prime Minister's freedom of manoeuvre

limited by the out-of-office parties and by his own back-benchers? How vulnerable is a Prime Minister at the head of a minority government? In the parliamentary battles what weapons does the Prime Minister have at his disposal? These particular questions will be examined in the next two sections of this chapter.

THE PRIME MINISTER AND HIS BACKBENCHERS

The 1974 dissolution of Parliament was only the sixth time since 1867 that a Canadian Prime Minister had felt compelled to resign or seek a dissolution of Parliament as a result of a setback in Parliament. Macdonald resigned in 1873 when his government was deserted by some of its backbenchers and faced defeat at the end of the Pacific Scandal debate. Laurier in 1911 dissolved Parliament in the face of weeks of filibustering by the Conservative Opposition, and some of his own Liberal backbenchers, against the government's trade agreement with the U.S.A. Mackenzie King in 1926, facing certain parliamentary defeat, resigned when the Governor General refused to grant him a dissolution. Meighen in 1926, Diefenbaker in 1963, and Trudeau in 1974 sought a dissolution after their governments had suffered major parliamentary defeats.

On no other occasion since 1867 has a Canadian Prime Minister felt obliged to resign or seek a dissolution as a result of events in Parliament. Even on these six occasions there were "extenuating circumstances". King, Meighen, Diefen-baker, and Trudeau were at the head of minority governments, and their parliamentary downfall came because, for once, the out-of-office parties coalesced against them. Laurier in 1911, with an overall majority and two years of the Parliament still to run, could have persevered against the filibuster, and he sought a dissolution only because he was confident of winning the election. In the event, he miscalculated badly and lost the election by a wide margin. This leaves only Macdonald's resignation in 1873 as an example of a Canadian Prime Minister at the head of a government with an overall majority being forced to resign because of the defection of some of his own backbenchers. And this was more than a century ago when party alignments were much less firm than they are today. Why have there been so few occasions when a government has had to resign or seek an early dissolution?

a. Backbench Discipline

The traditional interpretation of the security of a government's parliamentary majority is that backbenchers avoid rebellion because they fear the consequences for themselves or for their party. An MP cannot be expelled from Parliament, but he can be ostracised from his party through the withdrawal of the Whip. In the short term this means that he is denied access to the centres of power, and loses the ability to influence party policy. In the longer term, ostracism will make it difficult (though certainly not impossible) for him to secure re-election to Parliament. Even if his constituency party continues to back him, the Prime Minister, other ministers, and the national party-machine are unlikely to support his re-election.

If he is not deterred by thoughts of these personal consequences, a potential rebel may be deterred by the possible effects upon the party. Although there is little hard evidence either way, it is generally assumed that open dissent within a party's ranks is electorally damaging to it. More than this, however, in the most extreme circumstances rebellion could lead either to the resignation of the government and the accession of the Opposition to power, or to a dissolution of Parliament and the possibility of the defeat of the MP or of the party as a whole.

The implication of these considerations is that the pressures for conformity upon government backbenchers are such that they dare not rebel. Open rebellion thus becomes a "Doomsday Weapon" which cannot be used because the consequences would be so devastating as to be unacceptable to the rebel. This interpretation of the pressures that determine backbenchers' behaviour, however, has to be modified by a further basic consideration. The Prime Minister recognizes just as well as his backbenchers the dangers to the government that are inherent in intra-party conflict. Indeed, the Prime Minister has *more* to lose from a resignation or a dissolution of Parliament than have backbench MPs, and a Prime Minister's sense of self-preservation is at least as well-developed as that of his backbenchers. It is a mistake, therefore, to assume that in disputes between a government and its backbenchers it will always be the backbenchers who will feel obliged to give way. The real basis of harmonious relations within the parliamentary party is a balance of influence between ministers and backbenchers. A Prime Minister has to know how far the bonds of personal and party loyalty can be stretched, and must refrain from pushing forward with policies that will snap these bonds. If a government is faced by a rebellion of its backbenchers on the floor of the House or in committee, this is an indication, not that backbenchers have suddenly found some courage, but that the normal processes of consultation between ministers and backbenchers have failed, for once, to produce a compromise acceptable to both sides. The absence of such rebellions is an indication, not that caucus is utterly compliant, and will accept any policy that the government thrusts at it, but that the government has recognized what caucus will and will not accept and has trimmed its policies accordingly.

Thus, in effect, the government's own backbenchers, rather than the official Opposition, perform the role that in the American system is performed by Congress as a whole—the role of bargaining with the executive in order to achieve concessions on policy. In the Canadian parliamentary system, opposition to the government by the out-of-office parties is largely ineffective as a means of wringing policy concessions from the government. Opposition by the government's own backbenchers, on the other hand, can be effective as a means of influencing policy outputs, as they have the power, ultimately, to overthrow the government, or at the very least to make life difficult for it by sowing discord at all levels of the party. Thus the relationship between Prime Minister and caucus is that of two negotiators, each with bargaining weapons, but each with a vested interest in preserving harmony and achieving a concensus that will keep the party in office. MPs are concerned with exerting influence within the party, not with wrecking it. Equally, the Prime Minister and his ministers are anxious to reconcile differences within the party and prevent MPs from withdrawing their support from the government.

The main forum for this exercise in reconciling attitudes is the caucus meeting, attended by the Prime Minister and other ministers, but chaired by a backbench MP. Caucus meets at least weekly when Parliament is in session, and invariably attendance is high. MPs also meet in provincial or regional groups, in some cases (as with the Ontario Liberals) weekly, and in other cases once or twice a month. A caucus meeting serves four main functions. First, it provides a formal stage for the expression of backbench opinions. The expression of discontent can in itself be therapeutic for backbenchers. More than this, however, it provides the Prime Minister with a sounding-board, indicating the nature and extent of backbench discontent. Backbench wisdom, as expressed in caucus meetings can even contribute to the greater success of a policy.

Second, a caucus meeting gives the Prime Minister and his ministers an opportunity to provide the party with information about government activities. This is far from being the only channel through which the party can be kept informed, but it is a convenient gathering for this purpose. Often the meeting will develop into a question and answer session. Lester Pearson used to welcome this:

> [in caucus meetings] I used to encourage the frankest kind of questioning, however critical. That helped, I hope, to estab-lish and maintain a leader's position with his parliamentary colleagues.[3]

Again, such an exercise can be therapeutic for MPs and in-formative for the Prime Minister and his ministers, indicating just how much of a credibility gap is building up between the government and the party.

Third, caucus meetings provide the Prime Minister and his ministers with an arena in which backbenchers can be per-suaded to support government policies. While Mackenzie King often spoke of caucus as a consultative body that reflected public opinion, in practice he used caucus meetings to try to persuade his supporters to accept policies that had been agreed upon in Cabinet. Here, then, as in the electoral arena, the Prime Minister has to practice the art of public persuasion.

Fourth, caucus meetings fulfil a legitimizing function, enabling intra-party democracy to be seen to be done. In effect, the consideration of policies in caucus provides an official stamp of approval. It enables the government to claim that due process of consultation has taken place. This can make it easier for the Prime Minister to secure acceptance for his policies among the party outside Parliament and among the public at large. More than this, it helps to legitimize the MPs' role, indicating to constituents, provincial party leaders, and group clients that backbenchers are involved in policy-making processes. It thereby provides status for MPs and a degree of comfort for those they represent.

Allan Kornberg, as part of his study of attitudes and behaviour in the 1962-63 Parliament, gathered evidence of what MPs saw to be the main function of caucus meetings.[4] Of the MPs interviewed, most (64 per cent) saw caucus meetings primarily as a means of devising parliamentary tactics and strategies. Another 20 per cent regarded them as a mechanism for achieving agreement on policy, and 13 per cent as a forum for the expression of grievances. This marked emphasis on "tactics and strategies" can perhaps be explained, in part at least, by the particular nature of the politics of the short 1962-63 Parliament, in which the main concern of all parties was with the death throes of the minority Conservative government. Nevertheless, the vast majority of MPs were prepared to attribute some role to caucus: only 3 per cent felt that caucus performed no real function.

David Hoffman and Norman Ward, in their 1965 survey of MPs' attitudes for the Royal Commission on Bilingualism and Biculturalism, also produced evidence on this question.[5] Some of their findings are shown in Table 6:1. The data indicates clearly that government backbenchers are less inclined than Opposition MPs to regard caucus's function as being that of making policy or devising strategy, and are more inclined to see it as a forum for "letting off steam" or "communicating information". It seems that the further a party is removed from experience or prospects of office, the more the emphasis is placed upon caucus' strategy-making and policy-making roles, with NDP and Social Credit MPs being particularly concerned with these functions.

For government backbenchers, of course, it is difficult to compartmentalize completely the various caucus functions listed above or shown in Table 6:1. The expression of dissent, for example, and the two-way communication of information and

Table 6:1

BACKBENCHERS' VIEWS OF CAUCUS FUNCTIONS

Response to question: "What do you see as the two main functions of your party caucus?"

	To let off steam %	To communicate information %	To devise party strategy %	To devise party policy %
Govt. backbenchers	57	87	13	21
Opp. backbenchers:				
PC	27	32	43	56
NDP	0	22	78	89
Social Credit	0	20	100	60
Créditistes	17	17	67	50

SOURCE: Based on Table in J. D. Hoffman and N. Ward, *Bilingualism and Biculturalism in the Canadian House of Commons*, (Ottawa: Queen's Printer, 1970), p. 163.

attitudes between front and backbenches, can lead indirectly to modifications in government policies and strategies. Certainly, while Hoffman and Ward found that many backbenchers, and government backbenchers in particular, were unhappy about their policy-making opportunities,[6] there was overwhelming agreement among government and Opposition backbenchers alike that caucus *was* an arena in which policy could be influenced: 86 per cent of Liberal and Conservative MPs, and 89 per cent of NDP MPs, rejected a statement put to them that "caucus is not a place for influencing policy".[7]

Hoffman and Ward also found evidence that under Lester Pearson and Pierre Trudeau the Liberal caucus has been much more directly involved in policy-making than it was under Mackenzie King or Louis St. Laurent.[8] Pearson encouraged the full discussion of policy in caucus, and made greater use of committees of caucus than had King or St. Laurent.[9] Typically, perhaps, Trudeau introduced greater formality into caucus proceedings. He enforced the practice of having a strict agenda for each meeting, with a pre-arranged list of speakers, each one limited to a three-minute contribution. He also established the principle that the government's legislative proposals be submitted to caucus at least a month before being presented to Parliament.

As well as formal meetings of caucus, of course, MPs have other, less formal means of making their views known to the Prime Minister. The Whips are a key channel of communication between the front and back benches. Too often the Whips are depicted purely in a policing role. They are also honest brokers, however, who pass on to ministers information about backbench opinions and reactions. MPs can also have contacts with the Prime Minister and other ministers at the personal level, through chance encounters in the corridors, restaurants, and rooms of Parliament Hill, through letters or memoranda, or through more formal deputations. Less directly, an MP can attempt to use his provincial party or constituency party machine to pressure the government. Ultimately if these channels of intra-party communication prove to be unsatisfactory, the MP can turn to the parliamentary and public platform. Through the formal procedures of debate and question in the House, through the mass media, or through public outlets, the MP can seek popular backing for his point of view.

b. Prime-Ministerial Resources

In confrontations with his backbenchers, what bargaining weapons does the Prime Minister possess, and what pressures can he exert? Many of the factors that were quoted in Chapter Five as being used to influence ministerial behaviour can be used also to influence backbench behaviour. Patronage, concessions on policy, and the adjustment of the parliamentary timetable to accommodate items of concern to backbenchers, are prominent among the Prime Minister's weaponry. Because ministers are drawn exclusively from Parliament, and almost exclusively from the Commons, a large proportion of Government party MPs will be office-seekers. Hoffman and Ward found that a third of Liberal (that is, Government party of the day) backbenchers admitted to being interested in the prospects of a Cabinet post, and another quarter expressed interest in some other public office.[10] It is not unreasonable to assume that many of those who do not *admit* to having ministerial ambitions nevertheless covet office, and will adjust their behaviour towards that end.

There is also some survey evidence of the extent to which MPs value the opportunity to influence the content of legislation. Kornberg found that approximately three-quarters of Canadian MPs had goals that were linked with legislative policies,[11] while Hoffman and Ward found that half of English-speaking backbenchers, and two-thirds of French-speaking backbenchers, classed themselves as "lawmakers" (that is, they saw their role to be that of making and amending legislation).[12]

Potential rebels can be given special attention by the Prime Minister. In the first Parliament of Confederation John A. Macdonald had to nurture his parliamentary support very carefully, as the bonds of party loyalty were weaker than they are today, and he was heading, in effect, a coalition ministry. Macdonald kept on his desk a list of MPs with supporters ticked in blue, opponents in red, and the "doubtfuls" left blank. These uncommitted MPs would be carefully wined and dined, invariably with gratifying results for the government's majority.[13] Subsequent Prime Ministers have used similar techniques to flatter MPs into conformity.

The Prime Minister's personal interest is often most welcome in an electoral context. Trudeau after the 1968 election, Diefenbaker after the 1958 election, and Mackenzie King for most of his prime-ministerial career, could capitalize on the undoubted fact that many MPs owed their parliamentary seats to the electoral appeal exerted by the Prime Minister. MPs who are in danger of losing their seats may require special assistance in their campaign from the Prime Minister and the party machine. Those who do not conform can be denied this assistance. Clearly, however, while one or two MPs may be regarded as expendable, there is a limit, with a Commons of just 264 members, to the number of MPs that the Prime Minister can afford to abandon in this manner.

The granting or withholding of such prime-ministerial favours can be used to deter backbench rebellions. More generally, the Prime Minister can make appeals for loyalty "in the national interest" or "the party interest". In such appeals the Prime Minister can draw upon his personal prestige as national leader and party leader. In this his position is enhanced by the fact that he was selected to be the party leader by a national Convention rather than by caucus. This gives the Prime Minister a direct link, over the heads of caucus, with the party outside Parliament. Mackenzie King, for example, frequently used his selection by the party's grass roots as a status symbol in conflict with caucus.[14] More than this, however, the complicated process that is involved in organising a leadership Convention means that it is difficult for a caucus coup to take place (as Diefenbaker's opponents discovered to their cost in 1963).[15]

The Prime Minister's negotiating position with caucus is also strengthened by the relatively low status of Parliament as an institution, and of MPs as individuals. The Canadian Parliament lacks national recognition and sympathy. Perhaps it suffers from the proximity of the much more powerful and prestigious United States Congress, and from the inability of the layman (and of many politicians, journalists, and political scientists) to appreciate that Parliament is *not* Congress, and that the two bodies perform different roles within their respective constitutions. The British Parliament also suffers from comparisons with Congress, but unlike the Canadian Parliament it has history on its side, in the form of the dubious view that if it has survived from the thirteenth century it *must* be significant. Such a view is not readily transportable across the Atlantic.

The twin principles of collective responsibility and Cabinet secrecy mean that backbenchers are faced by a united front of Cabinet ministers, and are not informed of the differences of opinion that may have been expressed before the Cabinet reached its decision. MPs are thus prevented from capitalizing on the divisions that inevitably exist among ministers. In contrast, caucus itself will rarely be united. Inevitable ideological, regional, and personality differences exist within the caucus, and these can be exposed and exploited in debate. A favourite tactic of Mackenzie King, for example, was to encourage a full expression of caucus opinion about proposed government policies, and then underline the differences of opinion as a means of justifying the government's own view.

Pierre Trudeau's crudely made point that away from Parliament Hill MPs are "just nobodies" touched on the undoubted fact that, in general, MPs lack credibility and public esteem. The fairly rapid turnover of MPs contributes to this situation. Generally a third to a half of those elected at a general election will have no legislative experience, and only a tenth or less will have ten years' experience.[16] A variety of factors contribute to this high turnover rate. Many of those who enter the Commons regard parliamentary service as only a brief interlude in a career in business or in provincial politics. Some of those who would like to retain their seats are not re-adopted by the local party, while the relative shortage of "safe" seats in Canada means that in every general election a number of MPs are defeated at the polls.[17] In the recruitment of ministers less emphasis is placed on the desirability of long parliamentary experience than is the case, say, in Britain. Of Liberal ministers appointed in the 1921-70 period, a third had spent less than a year in Parliament when appointed, and half had spent less than five years in Parliament.[18] Clearly, however, it is arguable whether MPs leave Parliament because in the selection of ministers they have been passed over in favour of newcomers to Parliament, or whether newcomers are recruited because there are so few long-serving MPs.

One consequence of this rapid turnover is that MPs hold the job for too short a period to acquire confidence and competence in their role. As Dawson and Ward point out:

> Too much time must be spent by new members in acquiring familiarity with their work; too large a proportion of members will be forced through ignorance to give automatic acquiescence to the proposals of their leaders; valuable experience and knowledge melt away when they are beginning to yield maximum return.[19]

Kornberg argues that the rapid turnover of MPs also contributes to caucus harmony by eliminating potential rebels before they have an opportunity to come into conflict with party leaders over policy. Kornberg claims:

> The high level of attrition characteristic of the Canadian system, although it may be disfunctional in certain respects, helps to insure that most of those who are likely to become disenchanted and frustrated with their party roles are returned to the status of ordinary citizens before that frustration becomes intense enough to threaten the viability of the responsible party system.[20]

Again, MPs who are vulnerable to electoral defeat might be expected to be less nationally minded, and more constituency minded and parochial, than MPs whose electoral base is sound. Certainly, Hoffman and Ward found that Canadian MPs were not particularly nation-oriented, with only a quarter of back-benchers regarding the nation (rather than the constituency or the province) as the focus of their activities.[21] To this extent (as J. A. A. Lovink has argued)[22] a hardening of electoral loyalty in Canada, and a consequent growth in the number of safe seats, might, ironically, strengthen Parliament in its relationship with the government.

Thus, the relative low status of Parliament as an institution and of MPs as individuals; the general appeals for backbench support that a Prime Minister can make from his prestigious position as national and party leader; the more specific rewards in terms of posts, policies, and prime-ministerial attention that can be granted or withheld—all of these things strengthen the Prime Minister's hand in his dealings with his backbenchers. They help him to retain his position as Prime Minister *and* secure caucus acceptance of his policies. The mistake is frequently made, however, of lumping these two things together. From the unarguable fact that Prime Ministers have not been overthrown by caucus rebellions, the argument sometimes slides into the assumption that Prime Ministers are able to persuade caucus to accept all policies unquestioningly. "Security of tenure", however, is *not* the same thing as "security of policies". Indeed, Prime Ministers avoid backbench rebellions precisely because concessions are made on policy. Compromise with backbench views is the price that is paid for security of tenure. If the Government party does not have an overall majority, this process of compromise has to be extended also to the minor parties.

THE PRIME MINISTER AND THE MINOR PARTIES

Of Canada's thirty general elections, seven have been "indecisive" in the sense that no party won an overall majority (See Table 6:2). The Parliaments that followed these seven elections were all shorter than average. The 1921-25 Parliament, when the Liberal government was only just short of an overall majority, lasted for almost four years, but the other six were all dissolved within two and a half years. In all, the seven Parliaments add up to a total of just thirteen years, so that Canada's experience with minority governments has not been extensive. At the same time, seven and a half of these thirteen years have been since 1962, and five of the eight general elections in the 1957-74 period resulted in minority governments. Clearly, minority governments are much more likely to emerge in the multi-party politics of the post-1945 period than they were in the almost exclusively two-party politics of the first fifty years of Confederation.

Minority governments are generally seen as being inherently unstable. Certainly, the task of securing a parliamentary majority for government policies is made doubly difficult. As well as keeping his own backbenchers contented, the Prime Minister has to court the affections of the minor party or parties. The latter task will make the former much more difficult. Precisely because Canada has been governed by majority govern-

Table 6:2

PARTIES' SHARE OF SEATS IN "MINORITY" PARLIAMENTS

Election	Leading Party		Second Party		Third Party		Fourth Party*	
1921	Lib	49.4	Progs	27.2	Con	21.3	—	
1925	Con	47.3	Lib	40.4	Progs	9.8	—	
1957	Con	42.3	Lib	39.6	CCF	9.4	SC	7.2
1962	Con	43.8	Lib	37.7	SC	11.3	NDP	7.2
1963	Lib	48.7	Con	35.8	SC	9.1	NDP	6.4
1965	Lib	49.4	Con	36.6	NDP	7.9	SC	5.3
1972	Lib	41.2	Con	40.3	NDP	11.7	SC	5.8

*Excludes Independents and "Others"

SOURCE: J. M. Beck, *Pendulum of Power* (Scarborough: Prentice-Hall, 1968).

ments for the greater part of its history, minority governments when they do occur are seen as "abnormal" and lacking authority. The constitutional crisis of 1926, arising out of the country's first experience of minority government, left a fear that all minority governments are liable to such crises. But are minority governments necessarily so unstable?

A Prime Minister can adopt a variety of strategies in order to safeguard a minority government's parliamentary position. The most direct means of avoiding the risk of defeat are by curtailing the length of the parliamentary session and, when Parliament is in session, avoiding controversial measures. After the election of June 1962, for example, Diefenbaker did not summon Parliament until September 27, and then introduced only innocuous measures, postponing the consideration of issues that might unite the out-of-office parties. Analyses have been made of the length of sessions and the legislative output of different Parliaments.[23] These analyses indicate that when a minority government is in office the relative length of the sessions (as measured by the ratio of actual sitting-days to possible sitting-days) is generally lower than when a majority government is in office. They also indicate that the relative legislative load (as measured by the number of bills introduced per sitting) is generally lower for minority governments than for majority governments.

Clearly, however, there are limits to the practicality of these tactics. Parliament has to meet each year, and a certain amount of controversial business is bound to arise. Blatant attempts to gag the Opposition will prove counter-productive, and if the Opposition parties are sufficiently determined they will soon be able to manufacture a confrontation with the government. What is more, far from avoiding the introduction of legislation, a minority government will want to introduce measures with which to "buy" the support of the minor parties. In the 1921-25 Parliament, when the Liberal government was dependent on the Progressive Party for a majority, Mackenzie King introduced legislation to aid the Prairie farmers. Not only were the Progressive MPs bound to support such measures, but they also found it difficult to vote against so beneficent a government. This strategy was intensified after the 1925 election, and a Cabinet committee met regularly with the Progressive Party executive. The introduction of a bill to establish a Farm Loan Board, for example, was a direct result of Progressive Party pressure. The 1963-68 Pearson minority government, and the 1972-74 Trudeau minority government, adopted similar tactics, securing NDP support for extended periods by the simple expedient of appropriating measures from the NDP program. Medicare, universal pensions, and a federal labour code were adopted as Liberal policy in the 1960s after the NDP had championed the schemes. NDP influence was also apparent in the Trudeau government's legislation on pensions, foreign ownership, housing, and energy resources.

The Prime Minister's control of patronage can also be used to secure minor-party support. The ultimate use of this weapon would be to offer to bring the minor parties into a formal coalition government, but this has not been attempted on any of the occasions when the Prime Minister has lacked an overall majority. Less drastically, however, offers of ministerial posts can be made to individuals within the minor parties. T. A. Crerar, for example, as a leading Progressive MP in the 1921-25 Parliament, was tempted into the Liberal Party by King, and later became a Liberal Cabinet minister.[24] Posts at other levels can be offered to party officials and supporters.

The government's position will be helped if it is possible to play off one minor party against another. This, of course, will depend upon the relative strength of the parties, and the number of votes the government needs for an overall majority (see Table 6:2). In the 1925-26 Parliament the King government needed the support not just of the Progressives, but of the few independent MPs as well. In the 1972-74 Parliament the Liberals could survive with NDP backing, but Social Credit support alone was not enough. On other occasions the government's position has been stronger. The Liberals were only just short of an overall majority throughout the 1963-65 period, so that the government could get its majority with either NDP or Social Credit support; while in the 1921-25 Parliament the King government required the votes of only a few Progressive MPs. Diefenbaker's minority governments could just survive with support from either Social Credit or the NDP.

In some situations, then, a Prime Minister will be able to apply a strategy of divide and rule towards the other parties. In the 1962-63 Parliament Social Credit and the New Democrats voted together against the Diefenbaker government only twice, although one of these occasions was on the motion of censure that led to the government's fall. In the 1963-65 Parliament, Diefenbaker, as Leader of the Opposition, could not unite the Social Credit and NDP MPs behind him, and Social Credit voted with the Liberal government throughout the Parliament. On one occasion Diefenbaker accused the Liberal government of literally buying the support of the minor parties by proposing major salary increases for MPs.[25]

The potential unity of the Opposition parties is undermined by the fundamental fact that they are electoral rivals. The NDP as a quasi-Socialist party, and the Social Credit and Créditiste parties as right-wing protest movements, will have little in common in ideological terms. In the 1960s, the Conservative and Social Credit parties were rivals for the Prairie vote, and thus were as anxious to discredit each other as they were to mount joint attacks upon the government. Diefenbaker, as Leader of the Opposition, was liable to attack the New Democrat and Social Credit parties as vehemently as he attacked the government, and this made difficult the emergence of any united front.

The minor parties' desire for an election may be little greater than that of the government. There are two important factors involved here. In the first place, the main Opposition party may be regarded by the minor parties as a worse alternative than the established government. The Progressives in the 1920s, and the NDP in the 1960s, were somewhat closer in ideological terms, to the Liberals than to the Conservatives. With the Liberals in office they could expect to feel more sympathy for government proposals, and could expect a more sympathetic reaction to their own aims, than with the Conservatives in office. Secondly, the minor parties clearly benefit from a parliamentary situation in which they have a strong bargaining position, and they will be wary of precipitating an election that could produce a majority government. This factor will not apply, of course, if a minor party feels that it has a good chance of improving its position at an election. The precedents, however, are not encouraging for the minor parties. As indicated in Table 6:3, the minor parties have invariably lost ground at elections after periods of minority government. This may be a reflection of the difficulty a minor party can have in performing its parliamentary balancing act. It has to be seen to be making responsible use of its power, but equally it has to avoid appearing merely as a dupe of the government. As one political journalist depicted the difficulties of the NDP in the 1972-74 Parliament:

> . . . the rest of us have been treated to the spectacle of David Lewis thumbing his nose at Prime Minister Trudeau and slapping him on the back simultaneously.[26]

In an election that results from a government defeat at the hands of the combined Opposition parties, the minor parties can be blamed for subjecting the electorate to the tedium of yet another federal election. During the parliamentary crisis of February 1968, when the Pearson minority government faced the possibility of defeat on a motion of no confidence, the Créditistes rallied to the support of the government at the last

Table 6:3

CHANGE IN MINOR PARTIES' VOTE AT ELECTIONS
FOLLOWING A PERIOD OF MINORITY GOVERNMENT

Election	Percentage Rise or Fall in Vote Compared With Previous Election		
	Third Party		Fourth Party*
1925	Progressive	− 14.0	—
1926	Progressive	− 3.6	—
1958	CCF	− 1.2	Social Credit − 4.0
1963	NDP	− 0.4	Social Credit + 0.2
1965	NDP	+ 4.8	Social Credit − 3.5
1968	NDP	− 0.9	SC/Créds. − 3.2
1974	NDP	− 2.1	SC/Créds. − 2.6

*Excludes Independents and "Others"

SOURCE: J. M. Beck, *Pendulum of Power* (Scarborough: Prentice-Hall, 1968).

minute, largely because the Créditistes had the most to lose in an ensuing election.[27] In 1974 the NDP almost certainly suffered in the election from having precipitated it by withdrawing their support from the government over its economic policy.

Again, the lack of an overall majority provides the Prime Minister with alibis. He can attribute the inadequacies of his minority government to the "unstable" parliamentary situation. He can accuse the minor parties of undermining "strong government", and can claim that national problems would be more easily dealt with if only he had an overall majority in Parliament. The Liberals tended to argue this way in the 1960s. As Eugene Forsey pointed out (writing in 1964):

> During the election of April, 1963, Liberal speeches and editorials tended to depict minority government . . . as a nameless, faceless, horror, the political fate that is worse than death. The authors of these productions are now hard at work trying to prove themselves wrong.[28]

Ministers in a minority government may well believe this to be the case, but even if they do not they can still use the argument with effect in their electoral propaganda.

The notion that majority government is "normal" and intrinsically desirable is fairly well established in the popular consciousness of Canadians. The Constitutional crisis of 1926, arising as it did from the Liberal government's lack of an overall majority, no doubt contributes to this, at least at the elite level. In his surveys conducted during the 1968 campaign, John Meisel found that 70 per cent of his respondents saw the election of a government with an overall majority as being "important" or "very important".[29] Meisel concluded that:

> Our data certainly offer overwhelming evidence that Canadians do not like minority governments. This strong feeling on the part of so many Canadians can be interpreted as a powerful factor in the frequent election to office of the Liberals who, because of their broad electoral base and widespread appeal, are often given the best chance of winning a Parliamentary majority.[30]

There is some evidence that Canadians' distrust of minority governments was less intense in the mid-1970s than in the mid-1960s. Nevertheless, Canadian Institute of Public Opinion

(CIPO) surveys conducted during the 1972-74 Parliament found consistently that most electors preferred majority to minority government, and the 1974 post-election survey by Pammett *et al.* found that 55 per cent of the electorate favoured majority governments as against 28 per cent favouring minority governments.[31] While it seems that only a small proportion of those who voted Liberal in 1974 did so primarily because of the majority government issue, the relative importance of this group of electors is considerable, given that it required only a slight increase in the overall Liberal vote to produce a majority government in 1974.

In general, however, minority governments are in a much stronger position than is suggested by the surface antagonisms of parliamentary party relationships. Certainly, Canadian Prime Ministers who have found themselves without an overall majority have, for the most part, survived the experience well. Of the seven Parliaments in which there have been minority governments, four (1921-25, 1957-58, 1963-65, and 1965-68) were dissolved only because the Prime Minister sought an election, while in 1974 the Prime Minister probably welcomed the parliamentary setback that gave him an excuse to face the electorate at a relatively opportune time for his party. At elections after periods of minority government, Meighen in 1926 and Diefenbaker in 1963 were defeated, but King in 1925, Diefenbaker in 1958, Pearson in 1965, and Trudeau in 1968 and 1974 all led the Government party to victory, with all except King in 1925 achieving an improvement in the party's parliamentary position. As noted in Table 6:3, on the other hand, the third and fourth parties have almost always been punished by the electorate after holding the parliamentary balance of power.

Some parties and some Prime Ministers will be better suited to minority governments than will others. The Liberal Party's pragmatic approach to policy, and its proven ability to be all things to all men, are perhaps ideally suited to the politics of minority government. The social welfare policies introduced by the Pearson and Trudeau governments undermined the position of the NDP, just as the agricultural reform policies adopted by Mackenzie King in the 1920s undermined the Progressive

Party. King as the arch-compromiser and with his experience in labour relations, and Lester Pearson with his experience in international diplomacy, were ideally suited to lead minority governments. Pierre Trudeau, on the other hand, as a more abrasive political figure, was perhaps less temperamentally suited to the task, but he survived his eighteen-month dependence upon the NDP.

CONCLUSION

In this chapter attention has been focused upon the weapons that the Prime Minister can use in the parliamentary power game. As was emphasized at the beginning of the chapter, however, this has to be seen within the broad context of the government's ultimate answerability and responsibility to Parliament. Three final points need to be made to re-emphasize this. First, all too often parliamentary politics are presented as a simple confrontation between the government and "the" Opposition. It is clear, however that the Prime Minister and his ministers face within Parliament three distinct Opposition groups—the main out-of-office party; such other parties and independents as win seats; and the backbenchers of the government party. Whether or not the government has an overall majority, its own backbenchers are in the most potentially influential position of all. The Prime Minister must retain the loyalty of his backbenchers in order to survive from one election to another. Opposition from the out-of-office parties is official, public, and spectacular, being expressed openly across the floor of the House. Opposition from the government's own backbenchers, on the other hand, is unofficial, private, and unspectacular. Precisely because it is private and unspectacular it is all too easily underestimated.

Second, it is clear that the politics of minority government are not *fundamentally* different from those of majority government. A mistake that is made all too often is to assume that a Prime Minister whose party lacks an overall majority in Parliament is bound hand and foot, while a Prime Minister whose party does have a clear overall majority enjoys almost unlimited freedom of manoeuvre. Such an over-simplification is clearly based upon false premises. As Trudeau demonstrated in the 1972-74 Parliament, a Prime Minister at the head of a minority government has a variety of weapons that he can use to attract the support of the minor parties. At the same time, all Prime Ministers, whether or not they have an overall majority, find their freedom of action limited by a vast range of parliamentary and extra-parliamentary considerations. A Prime Minister survives and prospers according to his ability to come to terms with his Cabinet, his backbenchers, the party at large, the provinces, powerful interest groups, international pressures, and, ultimately, the electorate. The absence of an overall parliamentary majority merely adds a further group—the minor parties—to those whose attitudes have to be taken into consideration in the formulation of policies and tactics. The process of accommodation is thereby made more difficult for the Prime Minister, but the basic rules of the prime-ministerial power game remain unchanged.

Third, it may be noted that as far as President-Prime Minister and Congress-Parliament comparisons are concerned, the events in Ottawa and Washington in the summer of 1974 were highly instructive. In August 1974 Richard Nixon resigned as President of the United States as a result of political and judicial pressure that was exerted upon him by various forces, not least by Congress. In that same summer Pierre Trudeau *survived* as Prime Minister of Canada despite the clear parliamentary defeat that his government suffered on a motion of no confidence. In face of the parliamentary censure, Trudeau chose to dissolve Parliament rather than resign, and subsequently he was able to persuade the electorate to return his government to power with a greatly increased majority. At first sight these events seem to disprove one of the classical distinctions that is drawn between presidential and parliamentary systems—the traditional security of tenure enjoyed by a directly elected president, compared with the vulnerability of a Prime Minister who is accountable to Parliament. In fact, the events do more to prove than to disprove the traditional interpretation of President-Congress and Prime Minister-Parliament relationships. Even though the Trudeau government was returned to power at the 1974 election, the fact that the election had been precipitated by a parliamentary defeat for the government on a major item of policy indicates that Prime Ministers at the head of minority governments *are* ultimately vulnerable to parliamentary reversals. Equally, the Watergate affair demonstrated the very strength of a president's position. The remarkable thing is not that Richard Nixon eventually was forced to resign, but that he was able to survive for so long in the face of the threat of impeachment, the loss of his public credibility, and the pressures put on him by Congress, the judiciary, his own party colleagues, the press, and the public. It is safe to say that a Watergate-type scandal in a Canadian context, or in the context of any other parliamentary system with its basis of executive responsibility to the legislature, would have led to an early resignation by the Prime Minister as a result of a rebellion within the Cabinet or the caucus, or, if it was a minority government, through the withdrawal of minor-party support. This, however, touches on the broader question of a Prime Minister's overall security of tenure and this will be examined more fully in the concluding chapter.

NOTES

1. Quoted in T. A. Hockin, *The Apex of Power* (Scarborough: Prentice-Hall, 1971), p. 184.
2. Denis Smith, *President and Parliament*, paper presented to the Priorities for Canada Conference, Niagara Falls, October 1969. See above p. 2.
3. Hockin, *Apex of Power*, p. 194.
4. Allan Kornberg, *Canadian Legislative Behaviour* (New York: Holt, Rinehart and Winston, 1967), p. 132.
5. J. D. Hoffman and N. Ward, *Bilingualism and Biculturalism in the Canadian House of Commons*, a report to the Royal Commission on Bilingualism and Biculturalism (Ottawa: Queen's Printer, 1970).
6. Ibid., pp. 140, 154.
7. Ibid., p. 160.
8. Ibid., p. 161.
9. Hockin, *Apex of Power*, p. 149.
10. Hoffman and Ward, *Bilingualism and Biculturalism*, p. 128.
11. Kornberg, *Canadian Legislative Behaviour*, p. 145.
12. Hoffman and Ward, *Bilingualism and Biculturalism*, p. 85.

13. B. Hutchison, *Mr. Prime Minister 1867-1964* (Don Mills: Longmans, 1964), p. 20.
14. J. Lederle, "The Liberal Convention of 1919", *Dalhousie Review*, 1948, p. 86.
15. See below p. 145.
16. J. A. A. Lovink, "Is Canadian Politics Too Competitive?", *Canadian Journal of Political Science*, 1973, p. 369.
17. Ibid., p. 357.
18. J. C. Courtney, *The Selection of National Party Leaders in Canada* (Toronto: Macmillan, 1973), p. 157.
19. R. M. Dawson and N. Ward, *The Government of Canada* (Toronto: University of Toronto Press, 1967), p. 345.
20. Kornberg, *Canadian Legislative Behaviour*, p. 147.
21. Hoffman and Ward, *Bilingualism and Biculturalism*, p. 80.
22. Lovink, *CJPS*, 1973, p. 377.
23. Allan Kornberg and Lloyd B. Musolf, eds., *Legislatures in Comparative Perspective* (Durham, North Carolina: Duke University Press, 1970), pp. 107-8; R. J. Jackson and Michael M. Atkinson, *The Canadian Legislative System* (Toronto: Macmillan, 1974), pp. 161-3.
24. H. B. Neatby, *William Lyon Mackenzie King* (Toronto: University of Toronto Press, 1973), II: 17.
25. Quoted in P. C. Newman, *The Distemper of Our Times* (Toronto: McClelland and Stewart, 1968), p. 98.
26. Walter Stewart, *Maclean's*, December 1973, p. 6.
27. For an account of these events see R. M. Punnett, "The Parliamentary Crisis of 1968", *Parliamentary Affairs*, 1968-9, pp. 16-25.
28. Eugene Forsey, "The Problem of 'Minority' Governments in Canada", *Canadian Journal of Economics and Political Science*, 1964, p. 1.
29. John Meisel, *Working Papers on Canadian Politics* (Montreal: McGill-Queens University Press, 1972), p. 18.
30. Ibid., p. 54.
31. J. Pammett, et al., *The 1974 Federal Election: A Preliminary Report*, Carleton University Occasional Paper No. 4, p. 41.

7.   Full Circle: Retaining Office

"The perpetual re-eligibility of the President, I fear, will make an office for life, and then hereditary." So far, Thomas Jefferson's fears for the American presidency have proved groundless: it has not become the preserve of one family, and although a number of presidents have died in office, it has not become an "office for life" in the sense that Jefferson used the term. At one time, unwritten convention required that no one be elected to the presidency more than twice, and in 1951, after the convention had been breached by Franklin D. Roosevelt's exceptionally long tenure, the principle was enshrined formally in the 22nd Amendment to the Constitution.

No such restrictions, formal or informal, surround the office of Prime Minister of Canada. In July 1974 Pierre Trudeau won his third successive general election, thereby matching Mackenzie King's feat of the 1930s and 1940s, while prior to 1914 Sir John A. Macdonald and Sir Wilfrid Laurier each won four successive elections. A Prime Minister, then, enjoys the "perpetual re-eligibility" of which Thomas Jefferson was so wary, and can hold office indefinitely—provided that he avoids each of four natural hazards to which he is exposed. Most obviously, he has to avoid death, ill-health, a major personal scandal, or similarly fatal "accidents". Second, he has to beware of being deposed from the party leadership by a palace revolution. Third, he has to avoid a parliamentary defeat for his government, either through a withdrawal of support by his own party's MPs, or, if he heads a minority government, through the loss of minor-party support. Finally, he has to avoid defeat at a general election.

Canadian Prime Ministers have been comparatively successful in avoiding these pitfalls, in that they have enjoyed longer spells in office than have heads of government in many other countries. Some indication of this is given in Table 7:1. Of the thirteen countries listed in Table 7:1, only South African prime ministers in the 1900-74 period, and only Swedish prime ministers in the 1945-74 period, served for longer average

Table 7:1

PRIME-MINISTERIAL TENURES

	Number of Prime-Ministerial Terms*		Average Length of Each Term (in years)	
	1900-74	1945-74	1900-74	1945-74
Canadian Data				
Liberals	7(5)	4(4)	7.5	5.7
Conservatives	5(4)	1(1)	4.2	7.0
Total	12(9)	5(5)	6.2	6.0
Comparative Data				
Australia	26(21)[a]	8(7)	2.9	3.8
Britain	21(16)	8(8)	3.5	3.8
Ireland	9(6)[b]	8(5)	5.8	3.8
New Zealand	16(15)	7(6)	4.6	4.3
South Africa	8(7)[c]	5(5)	8.0	6.0
U.S.A. (Presidents)	13(13)	6(6)	5.7	5.0
Belgium	32(24)	16(11)	2.3	1.9
France	84(46)	30(23)	0.8	1.0
Germany	26(24)	5(5)	2.9	6.0
Italy	38(28)	19(14)	1.9	1.5
Netherlands	23(19)	12(11)	3.2	2.5
Sweden	27(21)	3(3)	2.7	10.0

*A "term", as used here, means an unbroken spell in office, which (as with Mackenzie King 1935-48) may extend over a number of Parliaments. Some Prime Ministers held office more than once: the figure in brackets is the number of Prime Ministers, and the main figure is the total number of prime-ministerial terms.
[a] The period is 1901-74.
[b] The period is 1922-74.
[c] The period is 1910-74.

SOURCE: Comparative data from R. Bidwell, *Guide to Government Ministers* (London: Cass, 1973) (updated from Keesings' Archives).

terms.[1] The Canadian terms are long in comparison with those of presidents of the U.S.A. or Prime Ministers of other Anglo-American countries such as Australia, Britain, Ireland, and New Zealand, but are especially long in comparison with those of Prime Ministers in continental European countries. While Canada has had nine Prime Ministers since 1900, serving average terms of over six years, Italy has had twenty-eight Prime Ministers serving less than two years per term, and France has had forty-six, serving less than a year per term. Belgium, Sweden, Germany, and the Netherlands also have had twice as many Prime Ministers as Canada this century.

Average figures for prime-ministerial terms, of course, can hide wide variations between individuals. The fifteen Canadian Prime Ministers can be divided into three broad groups on the basis of their number of years in office. The "big three", King, Macdonald, and Laurier, are in a class of their own, with tenures of twenty-two, twenty, and fifteen years respectively. King won a total of five general elections in this time, Macdonald six, and Laurier four. Between them they held office for fifty-seven out of the first eighty-one years of Confederation. Laurier's was the longest unbroken term, although King with one spell of thirteen years, and Macdonald with one of twelve and a half years, ran him close. At the other extreme, the "small five" (Meighen, Thompson, Abbott, Bowell, and Tupper) each served for less than two years, with Tupper's ten weeks being the shortest term.

Between these two extreme groups, seven Prime Ministers have held the post for between five and ten years. Borden and St. Laurent served for eight and a half years, and Mackenzie, Bennett, Diefenbaker, and Pearson for around five years. Trudeau, in office since 1968, would have to remain in office until 1983 in order to pass Laurier's record continuous term, and would have to survive until 1990 (by which time he would be seventy-one) to pass King's overall record of twenty-two years as Prime Minister.

It is clear that the length of a Prime Minister's period in office may bear little or no relationship to the expectations that surround his accession. The Conservatives under Diefenbaker in 1958 got 53 per cent of the popular vote and won more than three-quarters of the seats in the Commons, but at the election at the end of the Parliament the government was unable to retain an overall majority. Laurier, in contrast, crept into office in 1896 on the basis of an election in which his party won a majority of seats in only two provinces and secured one per cent *fewer* votes than the Conservatives, but he remained in power for fifteen years, winning three more elections in the process. Again, the seventy-year-old Senator Abbott was recognized by all (including himself) to be merely a stop-gap when he became Prime Minister in 1891. John Thompson, on the other hand, was widely regarded as being, at forty-eight, the new white hope of the Conservative Party when he succeeded Abbott eighteen months later, but Thompson's sudden death meant that his premiership lasted only a few months longer than Abbott's.

THE FOUR PITFALLS

Given the comparatively long terms served by Canadian Prime Ministers, what factors have brought about their eventual retirement? Abbott, Borden, King, and Pearson managed to avoid each of the four pitfalls mentioned at the beginning of the chapter, and chose their own time to retire gracefully. The others, however, left office in unhappy circumstances (see Table 7:2). Macdonald and Thompson died in harness. On twelve other occasions the Prime Minister was removed from office by his Cabinet colleagues, by Parliament, or by the electorate. Mackenzie Bowell resigned in 1896 as a direct result of a Cabinet revolt against his leadership. In January 1896 seven of his Cabinet resigned in protest at his ineffective handling of the Manitoba schools issue.[2] When Bowell tried to replace the seven ministers they successfully picketed the potential replacements. Bowell offered to resign, but the Governor General (Lord Aberdeen) would not agree to this as he was opposed to the only possible successor, Sir Charles Tupper. Eventually, however, Bowell and the Governor General gave way in face of the weight of Cabinet and party opinion against them. The seven ministers were accepted back into the Cabinet, and Bowell remained as Prime Minister only

Table 7:2

PRIME-MINISTERIAL ENTRANCES, TENURES, AND DEPARTURES

FEDERAL PREMIERSHIP

Method of Entry		Tenure, in years		Cause of Departure
Appointed at Confederation	Macdonald 1867	12½	Macdonald 1891	Died in office
		2	Thompson 1894	
Direct Entry — succeeded someone from the same party	Abbott 1891	1½	Abbott 1892	Voluntary retirement for reasons of age or ill-health
	Thompson 1892	8½	Borden 1920	
	Bowell 1894	13	King 1948	
	Tupper 1896	5	Pearson 1968	
	Meighen 1920			
	St Laurent 1948			
	Trudeau 1968			
		1½	Bowell 1896	Cabinet coup
Indirect Entry — became party leader in Opposition, and became Prime Minister when government resigned after —	Laurier 1896	6	Macdonald 1873	Government defeat in Parl.
	Borden 1911	4½	King 1926	
	King 1921			
	Bennett 1930			
	Diefenbaker 1957			
	Pearson 1963			
a) election defeat		5	Mackenzie 1878	Electoral Defeat
b) Parl. defeat	Mackenzie 1873	6 wks.	Tupper 1896	
		15	Laurier 1911	
		1½	Meighen 1921	
		3 mths.	Meighen 1926	
Re-Entry—regained power when govt. resigned after —	Macdonald 1878	5	Bennett 1935	
	King 1926	8½	St. Laurent 1957	
a) election defeat	King 1935	5½	Diefenbaker 1963	
b) Parl. defeat	Meighen 1926	4	King 1930	

until Tupper could be brought back from London (where he was serving as High Commissioner) to take over and lead the government into a general election — which it duly lost.

There have been other attempted coups. Israel Tarte, for example, sought to replace Laurier by building up his own following in the Cabinet, but to no avail.[3] John Diefenbaker was almost overthrown in 1963 through a revolt by some of his ministers, but the attempt was foiled when caucus rallied to his support.[4] The only example of a successful Cabinet coup, then, was in 1896. Equally, only once, in 1873, has a Prime Minister at the head of a government with a clear parliamentary majority had to resign because it lost that majority between elections. In the unprecedented events of the summer of 1926, however, the minority Liberal government resigned after King's clash with the Governor General, and the minority Meighen Conservative government that replaced it was soon defeated in the Commons and lost the consequent election.[5]

On nine occasions the Prime Minister's resignation resulted from defeat at the polls. On each of the nine occasions the Prime Minister resigned without waiting for Parliament to meet. This pattern was set in 1878. Mackenzie's Liberal government was soundly beaten in the election, securing only half as many seats as the Conservatives. Mackenzie resigned at once, and Macdonald was installed before Parliament met. Subsequently, Tupper in 1896, Laurier in 1911, Meighen in 1921 and 1926, King in 1930, and Bennett in 1935 all resigned before meeting Parliament when the election gave the Opposition party a clear overall majority of seats. On two further occasions, following the 1957 and 1963 elections, when the main Opposition party won more seats than the Government but did not have an overall majority, the Prime Minister again resigned without meeting Parliament. St. Laurent in 1957 and Diefenbaker in 1963 might have been justified in meeting Parliament to test whether the minor parties would allow them to remain in office, but instead they interpreted the election result as a rejection of their governments' records, and resigned without waiting for a parliamentary verdict.

Thus the electoral hurdle has been the most dangerous natural hazard faced by Canadian Prime Ministers, accounting for nine retirements as compared with only one because of a Cabinet revolt, and two through parliamentary defeats (plus the six through old age, ill-health, or death). Even so, the nine elections at which governments were defeated represent only a third of the total number of elections since 1867. The established government was returned to power with an increased majority at another third, and with a reduced majority at a further third (see Table 7:3). Thus a Prime Minister's vulnerability to electoral defeat should not be over-stated. Nevertheless, the electoral hurdle is a crucial one in a Prime Minister's battle to retain office.

In this century, of course, the Prime Minister's security of tenure has been based upon the ability of the Liberal Party to win elections, and upon the ability of Liberal Party leaders to avoid overthrow. The Liberals have been in office for more than 80 per cent of the time since 1935, and for 75 per cent of the time since 1896. Of the Liberal leaders in this period, Laurier died in office, King, St. Laurent, and Pearson retired more or less gracefully at a time of their own choosing, and Trudeau, as yet, has not encountered any serious challenge to his retention of the party leadership. Various factors account for the Liberal leaders' security of tenure. Youthfulness and good health have been important, in that since 1896 the Liberals have chosen either relatively young leaders (Laurier, King, and Trudeau were all in their forties when selected), or older leaders (St. Laurent and Pearson were both in their sixties when chosen) who subsequently proved to be fairly durable. Again, since the adoption of the Convention system of selecting leaders the task of replacing an incumbent Prime Minister has been made doubly difficult. As noted in Chapter Three, the leadership Convention system frees the leader from exclusive dependence upon his parliamentary colleagues, in that a Cabinet or caucus coup is not enough, in itself, to unseat him. What is more, the cumbersome nature of the Convention process means that it is much more suitable for use in the comparative leisure of Opposition than in the hurly-burly of office.

The principle of success breeding success also helps to explain why the Liberals have changed their leaders so infre-

Table 7:3

TIMING AND OUTCOME OF CANADIAN
FEDERAL GENERAL ELECTIONS*

| Result of Election | Year in which Parliament was Dissolved | | | | | | Total |
	1st	2nd	3rd	4th	5th	Full Term	
Government returned with increased maj.	1958	1874 1974	1965 1968	1904 1949	1900 1940	1917+	10
Government returned with reduced maj.				1882 1908 1925	1972 1887 1891 1953 1962 1972	1945	10
Government defeated	1926 1963		1911	1921 1930 1957	1878	1896 1935	9
Total	3	2	3	8	9	4	29

*1867 election excluded.
+Parliament extended beyond its five year limit because of the war.

quently this century. It is clear from Table 7:4 that while party leaders have been fairly secure in their posts so long as their party was in office, they have been much less secure when their party was in Opposition. Both of the main parties have changed their leaders twice as often in Opposition as they have in office. This contrast between security in office and vulnerability in Opposition is all the more striking when it is realized that four of the seven changes of leader that have taken place in office occurred in the extraordinary Parliament of 1891-96, when the Conservatives, plagued by ill-luck and intra-party conflict, struggled to find a successor to John A. Macdonald. Clearly, then, party leaders' security of tenure is not something that is associated with the Liberal Party *per se*, but specifically with the Liberal Party *in office* — just as in the early decades

Table 7:4

REPLACEMENT OF LIBERAL
AND CONSERVATIVE PARTY LEADERS — 1880-1976

	Leader Replaced while the Party was:		
	a) In Office	b) In Opposition	
Liberal	1948	1880	1919*
	1968	1887	1958
Conservative	1891*	1901	1948
	1892	1927	1956
	1894*	1938	1967
	1896	1941	1976
	1920	1942	

*Indicates that the vacancy was caused by the death of the incumbent leader.

of Confederation it was associated with the Conservative Party *in office.*

It is beyond the scope of this book to attempt a detailed analysis of the reasons why the Liberals have held on to office for so great a part of this century. Clearly, however, of vital importance have been considerations such as the party's ideological flexibility and its "bicultural" image. Its ideological flexibility has enabled it to adapt its program so as to undermine the appeal of new movements such as the Progressives in the 1920s, the CCF in the 1930s and 1940s, and the NDP and Créditistes more recently. Its bicultural image has allowed it to retain a firm base in Quebec (winning an absolute majority of seats there in every election this century, apart from 1958) while also normally attracting substantial support in Ontario and other parts of English-speaking Canada. Also important has been its ability to produce leaders like Laurier, King, and Trudeau who (as discussed in Chapter Two) have exerted considerable personal electoral appeal, and have been "in tune with the national mood" of their period.[6] Again, the principle of success breeding success applies here also. The longer a party spends in office the more electoral capital it can make out of its rivals' inexperience and its own credentials as the normal party of government, while the party in power normally can time elections so as to increase its own chances of success. This all important question of the timing of elections, however, needs to be examined more closely: on nine occasions the choice of the election date sealed the Prime Minister's fate.

a. The Decision

Parliament is dissolved by the Governor General, acting on the advice of the Prime Minister, but to what extent is the decision to seek a dissolution a personal one for the Prime Minister, as opposed to a collective one for the Cabinet as a whole? A Privy Council Minute of October 1935 indicates that the decision is among the Prime Minister's *personal* prerogatives: "The following recommendations are the special prerogative of the Prime Minister: Dissolution and Convocation of Parliament. . . ."[7] The Prime Minister is free, of course, to seek such advice as he thinks fit, and there is evidence that on occasions the issue has been well aired in Cabinet. In October 1886, for example, Macdonald's Cabinet spent a long afternoon discussing possible election dates, and it was eventually agreed that the Parliament should be ended without another session.[8] Again, in October 1914 the Borden Cabinet debated whether an election should be held in order to capitalize on the sentiments aroused by the outbreak of war.[9] On other occasions the Cabinet has merely been "informed" by the Prime Minister of the decision he has made without any consultations with colleagues. In 1930 King decided in February to hold a spring election.[10] He told Lapointe and Dunning (the latter being asked to prepare a vote-catching budget), but the rest of the Cabinet was not told until late in March, and the public announcement was not made until May. Similarly, King merely informed his War Cabinet that he had decided to hold an election early in 1940, without waiting for a further full session of Parliament.[11]

Even when the matter is discussed in Cabinet, this does not mean that the final decision is removed from the Prime Minister. Borden overruled his Cabinet and caucus in deciding to seek a dissolution in 1917, rather than extend the life of the Parliament until after the end of the war.[12] A meeting of

Mackenzie King's Cabinet on July 27, 1925 indicated that a majority of ministers favoured an autumn poll, but the final decision in favour of the October election was taken by King himself.[13] Again Judy LaMarsh reveals that in 1965: "We held long, confused, and repetitive discussions at Cabinet every few days about the advisability of calling an election."[14] At a Cabinet meeting on September 1, 1965, ministers voted seventeen to four in favour of an autumn election.[15] Walter Gordon was particularly keen for an election, and promised to resign if the Liberals did not get an overall majority. The ministers expected Pearson to accept the majority view, but the *final* decision was made by Pearson two days later, in consultation with five of his closest personal confidants (Tom Kent, Keith Davey, Richard O'Hagen, Mary Macdonald, and Mrs. Pearson). Again, Trudeau discussed the possibility of a dissolution at his first Cabinet meeting in April 1968, and he also talked to the Liberal caucus about it. Afterwards, however, he commented to the press that "the decision must be made by me, not by the Cabinet."[16]

b. The Limitations on Choice

The conventions of the parliamentary system of government mean that provided he can maintain a majority in the Commons, the Prime Minister can seek a dissolution at any time within the five years of a Parliament's maximum life. This provides clear benefits for the Prime Minister and his party. The Prime Minister can use the threat of a dissolution as a weapon against dissidents within his own party (on the lines of "support this policy in Cabinet and the Commons or I will be obliged to seek a dissolution"). Again, speculation in the press about the possible date of a general election can demoralize the Opposition by indicating how much of the initiative rests with the government. It can also emphasize the importance of the Prime Minister's personal initiative. Most significantly of all, however, the astute choice of the election date can increase the government's chances of re-election. It is the Prime Minister's trump card in the battle to maintain his party in power, and represents a major advantage for the government over the out-of-office parties as compared with a system, like that of the U.S.A., in which election dates are fixed.

Nominally the Prime Minister can choose any year of the Parliament, and any month of the year, for the election. In reality, however, what practical considerations limit his choice? The Governor General, of course, has the constitutional right to refuse a request for a dissolution, and it is possible even today that a Governor General would exercise this right if a Prime Minister was blatantly opportunistic — perhaps, for example, requesting a further dissolution immediately after an election had produced an unfavourable result.[17] More importantly, the *public* reaction to the timing of the election is clearly all-important, so the Prime Minister has to have a reasonable "excuse" for seeking a dissolution. If he dissolves very early in the Parliament, he risks being accused of running away from the problems of government. If he waits until very late in the Parliament he will be accused of being afraid to face the electorate. Also, the longer he waits, the fewer his options. Some months of the year are less practical than others for electioneering. The winter months are normally considered to be unsuitable because of the weather and the stigma of seasonal unemployment. In the nineteenth century this seemed to matter less, in that in the 1867-1920 period forty-one per cent of all federal and provincial elections were held in the months November to March, compared with just fourteen per cent in the period since 1920.[18] There are also problems involved in having elections during the summer holiday months, when many people are away from their constituencies, although in this century there have been two July polls (1930 and 1974) and one August poll (1953). Again, the usual budget months of April and May are not particularly suitable, although the tactic of using tax cuts in the budget to sweeten the electorate means that a June poll can be favourable for the government.

Formal preparations for an election take at least two months, as the compilation of the electoral register begins only after the election is announced.[19] The periodic redistribution of riding boundaries can also limit the choice. In 1965 Lester Pearson had to decide whether to fight an election on the old, very out-of-date boundaries, or wait until November 1966 when the new maps would be ready. The Prime Minister has to be sure that his party is internally united and primed (financially, organizationally, and spiritually) for the fight. Lack of such preparedness was one of the major problems that Diefenbaker faced in 1963. Consideration must also be given to the business before Parliament, as if the dissolution comes in mid-session, legislation may be lost. The political scene has to be relatively crisis-free, although elections were held while the country was at war in 1917, 1940, and 1945 (with the government being returned to power on each occasion). Because of the problems involved in fighting an election at the height of the war, King ignored the advice of C. G. Power and others that the election be held in 1944.[20] The result was that in order to transact essential business, Parliament had to sit until just hours before its legal deadline of April 16, 1945.

None of these considerations apply, of course, if the Prime Minister loses control of the parliamentary situation. On four occasions Parliaments have had to be dissolved earlier than the Prime Minister would have liked because the government suffered a parliamentary defeat or setback. In 1911 the Opposition was so successful in filibustering the government's attempts to get parliamentary approval for a tariff reduction agreement with the U.S.A., that Laurier gave up the battle and asked for a dissolution.[21] In 1926 Meighen was obliged to seek a dissolution when his minority government was defeated in the Commons, as were Diefenbaker in 1963 and Trudeau in 1974. Of these four occasions, only in 1974 did the government retain office after the election. The 1872-74 Parliament also ended "early" when Macdonald, facing certain defeat in the Commons at the end of the Pacific scandal debate, decided to tender the government's resignation rather than seek a dissolution. Mackenzie became Prime Minister and was quickly granted a dissolution, which produced a big majority for the new Liberal government.

c. Dissolution Tactics

The practical limitations upon the Prime Minister's choice of election date are thus considerable. Provided that he can steer his way through these difficulties, however, what strategies are open to him? Very broadly he can adopt one of three alternatives. He can seek a dissolution early in the Parliament in a snap attempt to improve his government's position; let the Parliament run most of its course, but still retain some freedom of choice during the fourth or fifth year; or let the Parliament run its full course if the government's electoral prospects remain bleak. Mackenzie King, for one, had reservations about this third alternative:

> The uncertainties and inevitabilities which necessarily surround it should be avoided. . . . I believe the bolder course, and the wiser, is to choose one's own time within limits rather than be forced to go to the country at a given moment.[22]

In fact, only four Parliaments have run their full term (see Table 7:3). The 1896 dissolution was delayed by the government in an attempt (ultimately unsuccessful) to overcome the attempts of the Opposition, and some Conservative MPs, to wreck the government's policy over the Manitoba schools issue.[23] In 1935 Bennett tried to counter his government's unpopularity by delaying the dissolution as long as possible, and in 1945 the dissolution was delayed until the last possible moment in order that essential war business could be transacted. In addition, the Parliament elected in 1911 ran for almost six years, as a result of special legislation to meet the wartime emergency. These four "late" dissolutions led to defeats for the government in 1896 and 1935 (both peacetime), but victories for the government in 1917 and 1945 (both wartime), although the government's victory in 1917 was achieved, in part at least, by a cynical manipulation of the franchise.[24]

Three Parliaments in the 1950s and 1960s were dissolved before they had run three years by Prime Ministers at the head of minority governments seeking an overall majority, even though they had not suffered, and did not face, a specific parliamentary defeat. In 1958 (after the Parliament had run for less than a year) and in 1968 (after two and a half years)

Diefenbaker and Trudeau achieved the big election victories they were seeking, while in 1965 (again after two and a half years) Pearson improved his parliamentary position but just failed to get an overall majority.

Three-quarters of the Parliaments, however, have been dissolved during their fourth or fifth years. On some of these occasions, even though the Parliament was fairly well advanced, the Prime Minister took full advantage of good fortune that came his way. Macdonald's choice of an election date in 1882 was particularly delicate, because after a troubled Parliament, economic conditions were relatively booming, industrialists were once again prepared to finance the Conservative Party, and the census provided an excuse for a gerrymandered redistribution of seats.[25] Macdonald's astute timing was rewarded with a big victory, even though his overall majority was reduced. Even late in the Parliament the Prime Minister may be able to catch the Opposition by surprise, by dissolving slightly sooner than anticipated. Macdonald's choice of March for the 1891 election caught the Liberals off their guard. Sir Joseph Pope advised Macdonald to hold the election then, rather than later in the year, because "The CPR crowd simply can't let you lose, with all they have at stake; they will shell out as never before."[26] And they did, thereby assisting Macdonald to retain office. Again, the 1940 dissolution took the Opposition slightly by surprise. With the outbreak of war in 1939, King pledged that Parliament would meet for another session, even though it had entered its fifth year. In fact, the 1940 session lasted only a few days, after King had found an excuse for a dissolution in the Ontario legislature's condemnation of his handling of the war.[27] In 1949 St. Laurent also dissolved in mid-session, after a tour of the Western Provinces had indicated to him that the time was ripe for a Liberal election victory.[28]

As a Parliament approaches or enters its final year, and the government's electoral prospects seem bleak, the Prime Minister may choose to seek a dissolution, rather than wait until the bitter end, because he detects even darker clouds on the horizon. In 1887 the government was unpopular after the Riel affair, but Macdonald decided to face the electorate then because he anticipated that the situation was more likely to deteriorate than to improve.[29] In 1921 there was pressure on Meighen to postpone the "inevitable" Conservative electoral defeat, but he preferred to face the electorate even though the Parliament had a full year to run.[30] Similarly, in 1925 and 1930 King decided to risk an election on the ground that the Liberal prospects, though poor, were unlikely to improve.[31] Of these four examples, Macdonald's gamble in 1887 paid off, but on the other three occasions the government was defeated, or lost its overall majority. On such occasions the inevitable, but unanswerable, question is whether the defeat would indeed have been worse at a later date.

The Prime Minister may wait, if not to the bitter end of the Parliament, at least into the fifth year. Diefenbaker in 1962, and Trudeau in 1972, waited until the fifth year and were then returned to power, although they lost their overall majority. Macdonald waited almost to the legal limit of the first Parliament of Confederation, and was then returned to power with a reduced majority. Mackenzie in 1878, however, was not so fortunate. He favoured an election in June 1878, but the Quebec and Manitoba members of the Cabinet wanted a delay.[32] When the election was eventually held in September 1878, the Liberals lost. The three-month delay was recognized later to have been a major tactical blunder, as it allowed Macdonald to organize the Conservative Party in Ontario, where the election was effectively won and lost. Mackenzie acknowledged his error afterwards, observing plaintively to his biographers, a few weeks before he died, that "I made a mistake; I should have dissolved in June."[33]

CONCLUSIONS

Most Prime Ministers have been able to time things somewhat better than did Mackenzie in 1878. This question of timing is undoubtedly one of the factors that has contributed to the remarkable record of success that Canadian Prime Ministers have had in federal general elections. It is worth re-emphasizing that incumbent Prime Ministers in Canada have won more than twice as many elections as they have lost. What is more, four of the nine occasions when the Prime Minister did lead his party to electoral defeat were in the comparatively short period 1921-35. In the first fifty years of Confederation incumbent Prime Ministers lost only three elections (Mackenzie in 1878, Tupper in 1896, and Laurier in 1911), while over the last forty years they have lost only two (St. Laurent in 1957, and Diefenbaker in 1963) — and even on these two occasions the electorate denied the new government an overall victory. It is a sobering thought for the newly elected leader of the Progressive Conservative Party that not since King dumped Bennett so decisively in 1935 has a Leader of the Opposition succeeded in winning an overall majority of seats at a general election. Even so, taking the whole period since Confederation, electoral defeat has accounted for the removal of more Prime Ministers than have all the other natural hazards (Cabinet coups, parliamentary defeats, old age, death, and ill-health) put together. The picture that emerges, then, is one of considerable prime-ministerial security of tenure: Canadian prime ministers win most of the elections they fight, and, for the most part, avoid the other hazards that could cause their downfall between elections.

How does this final aspect of a Prime Minister's life-cycle fit in with the picture of prime-ministerial power that has been presented in earlier chapters? Aspects of Canadian government and politics which focus public attention upon the Prime Minister were highlighted in Chapter Two. The open and highly publicized processes through which the parties select their leaders; the conspicuous part that is played by the Prime Minister, and the other party leaders, in election campaigns; the importance, among the factors that attract votes to a party, of the appeal that is exerted by the leader; the tendency for the mass media to present political conflicts in terms of personalities; the Prime Minister's role as a national symbol, unrivalled by the Governor General, the Queen, or any other public figure — these several factors combine to make the Prime Minister, in the eyes of most Canadians, the personification of the national government. This view is compounded by the facts revealed in this chapter regarding the length of prime-ministerial tenures. Most Canadian Prime Ministers have been relatively secure in their posts, and thus have remained before the public gaze for long periods. The consequent impression of prime-ministerial invincibility gives added weight to the interpretation of the Canadian political system as one in which the Prime Minister reigns supreme.

Certainly, it must be acknowledged that there is no more important person in Canadian government and politics than the Prime Minister of the day. Individuals such as the Governor General, powerful Cabinet ministers, caucus faction leaders, influential civil servants, leaders of powerful interest groups, all have key roles to perform in the process of government, and in particular situations one or other of them may exert more influence than does the Prime Minister. Taking the process of Canadian government as a whole, however, none of these figures outstrips the Prime Minister in importance. Today, as in 1867, the Prime Minister stands as the single most important figure in the Canadian political process.

But does it follow from this that it is reasonable to describe the Canadian system of government as "prime-ministerial" or "presidential" in character? It has been emphasized throughout this book that such descriptions are *not* justified because of the fundamental distinction that exists between the seeming concentration of power in the hands of the Prime Minister of the day, and the realities of his position. Although there is no more important figure than the Prime Minister, although he is widely seen as personifying the Government of Canada, and although (on past performance) he is relatively secure in his post, he faces very real constraints in the execution of his functions. Among the more important of these constraints are: the considerations that limit the Prime Minister's choice of ministers; the difficulties involved in holding together a Cabinet that is constructed on the basis of the representation of conflicting interests; the problem of steering a government machine that grows ever larger and more complex; the difficulty of securing Cabinet approval of the policies he wishes to implement; and the need for him to come to terms with his own party's backbenchers, and sometimes also the minor parties, in order to preserve his government's majority in the Commons. Factors such as these amount to so formidable a limitation upon a

Prime Minister's freedom of action that it is fundamentally misleading to describe the Government of Canada as being essentially "prime-ministerial" or "presidential" in character. Nominally the Prime Minister is supreme; in reality there are distinct limits to his powers.

This overall conclusion needs to be qualified in three respects, however. In the first place, it has to be acknowledged that conclusions regarding the nature and extent of prime-ministerial power cannot be precise because so many of the most important factors involved defy quantitative measurement. Many of the workings of government are shrouded in secrecy, and even when this is breached by the probings of journalists and academic researchers, or by indiscreet biographies and autobiographies, little of the information that is thereby revealed lends itself to precise measurement by quantitative techniques. Reasonably precise measurements, of course, can be made of things such as the importance of the party leaders in determining electoral behaviour, the occupational and educational characteristics of Prime Ministers, the length of prime-ministerial tenures, or the variations in regional representation in the Cabinet under different Prime Ministers. It is not possible to measure with any degree of precision, however, crucial matters such as the nature of the Prime Minister's relations with his Cabinet colleagues; the manner in which the Cabinet and its committees arrive at decisions; the amount of influence enjoyed by the PCO and the PMO; the extent to which the Prime Minister bows before caucus or grass-roots pressure; or the extent to which the Prime Minister pays heed to the views of the Opposition parties. In these areas the commentator is obliged to present his observations in the form of qualified generalizations. Inevitably, therefore, the conclusions that are offered here regarding the nature and extent of prime-ministerial power are, for the most part, impressionistic and generalized.

Further, many of the general statements that are made about the Prime Minister's role have to be accompanied by the proviso that within the overall constraints that affect all Prime Ministers, there is room for varied interpretations of the role by successive Prime Ministers. Thus the manner in which a

Prime Minister performs certain tasks, his interpretation of the extent of his functions, and the degree of influence he can exert in particular situations, will all differ to some extent from one incumbent to the next. Pierre Trudeau, for example, has been much more "reformist" in his attitude toward the institutional machinery that surrounds the premiership than was, say, Louis St. Laurent. Equally, R. B. Bennett executed the Prime Minister's role of chairman of the Cabinet in a much more authoritarian manner than did Wilfrid Laurier, while John Diefenbaker adopted a much more presidential style of general-election campaigning than did Lester Pearson. There is considerable scope for innovation by a Prime Minister with a positive approach to his role: there is even greater scope for inactivity by a Prime Minister who chooses to adopt a largely passive approach. Such personal factors limit the validity of general conclusions about the office of Prime Minister.

Finally, it should be noted that the distinction between "prime-ministerial government" on the one hand and "cabinet government" on the other is really one of degree rather than of kind. Few, if any, of those who describe Canadian government as prime-ministerial in character would go so far as to claim that *all* power lies with the Prime Minister and that the Cabinet, caucus and bureaucracy are left with merely ceremonial functions to perform. Equally, few, if any, of those who question the prime-ministerial interpretation of Canadian government would deny that the Prime Minister is the central figure of Canadian government. Clearly, the government of Canada operates neither on wholly autocratic lines, in the sense of the Prime Minister monopolizing power in the manner of an hereditary despot, nor on wholly pluralistic lines, in the sense of power and influence being shared equally among a range of individuals and institutions. Rather, the debate is over the question of the precise extent to which the Prime Minister, in the execution of his functions, has to bow to the influences that can be brought to bear by the Cabinet, the bureaucracy, the caucus, the Opposition parties, the grass roots of the party, and other interests outside Parliament. The argument that has been developed here is that these pressures are so considerable that to describe the Canadian system as "prime-ministerial" or "presidential" in character encourages a misunderstanding of the limitations that surround the office of Prime Minister of Canada.

Canadian Prime Ministers survive and enjoy power only so long as they succeed in accommodating those with whom they are obliged to deal. A Canadian Prime Minister's position is not that of a medieval monarch secure in an hereditary right to rule, nor that of a modern military dictator, preserved in office by force of arms, nor that of a political-religious leader sustained by the spiritual devotion of his flock. (Even the Messiah-like attraction associated with Diefenbaker in 1958 and Trudeau in 1968 fell somewhat short of this.) The Prime Minister's position is not even that of an American president who knows that, short of assassination, or a once-in-a-century upheaval such as that which led to the resignation of Richard Nixon, he can retain his office from one election to the next. The Prime Minister is free from the ultimate danger of rebellion by his Cabinet, his caucus, the party outside Parliament, or the other political forces with which he deals, only so long as he is able to defuse potential revolutionary situations. The supreme skill that a Prime Minister has to possess is the ability to reduce to a minimum the limitations on his freedom of manoeuvre, but then to recognize and come to terms with the limitations that cannot be overcome. In the end, the exercise of prime-ministerial power lies in the art of living within the considerable constraints that are imposed by the realities of political life.

NOTES

1. A "term", as used here, means an unbroken spell of office, which may extend over a number of Parliaments.
2. For details of this episode see J. Schull, *Laurier: The First Canadian* (Toronto: Macmillan, 1965), pp. 307-11, and W. Stewart Wallace, *The Memoirs of the Rt. Hon. Sir George Foster* (Toronto: Macmillan, 1933), pp. 86-90.
3. O. D. Skelton, *Life and Letters of Sir Wilfrid Laurier* (London: Oxford University Press, 1922), II: 176-83.
4. P. C. Newman, *Renegade in Power: The Diefenbaker Years* (Toronto: McClelland and Stewart, 1963), p. 357.

5. For a recent comment on the King-Byng episode see J. E. Esberey, "Personality and Politics: A New Look at the King Byng Dispute", *Canadian Journal of Political Science*, 1973, pp. 37-55.
6. J. R. Mallory's phrase. See J. R. Mallory, *The Structure of Canadian Politics*, Mount Allison University Publications, No. 4, 1959, p. 25.
7. Privy Council Minute 3374 of October 25, 1935.
8. D. Creighton, *John A. Macdonald* (Toronto: Macmillan, 1955-6), II: 465.
9. Skelton, *Life and Letters of Sir Wilfrid Laurier*, II: 440.
10. H. B. Neatby, *The Lonely Heights* (Toronto: University of Toronto Press, 1963), p. 322.
11. J. M. Beck, *Pendulum of Power* (Scarborough: Prentice-Hall, 1968), p. 223.
12. H. Borden, ed., *Robert Laird Borden: His Memoirs* (London: Macmillan, 1938), II: 714.
13. Neatby, *The Lonely Heights*, p. 61.
14. Judy LaMarsh, *Memoirs of a Bird in a Gilded Cage* (Toronto: McClelland and Stewart, 1969), p. 73.
15. P. C. Newman, *The Distemper of Our Times* (Toronto: McClelland and Stewart, 1968), p. 243, and D. Smith, *Gentle Patriot: A Political Biography of Walter Gordon* (Edmonton: Hurtig, 1973).
16. *Globe and Mail*, April 22, 1968.
17. For the definitive discussion of this issue see Eugene Forsey, *The Royal Power of Dissolution of Parliament in the British Commonwealth* (Toronto: Oxford University Press, 1968).
18. J. Lightbody, "Swords and Ploughshares: The Election Prerogative in Canada", *Canadian Journal of Political Science*, 1972, pp. 287-91.
19. N. Ward, "The Representative System and the Calling of Elections", *Canadian Journal of Political Science*, 1973, pp. 655-60.
20. Beck, *Pendulum of Power*, p. 243.
21. Ibid., p. 123.
22. Neatby, *The Lonely Heights*, p. 60.
23. Beck, *Pendulum of Power*, p. 77.
24. For detailed comment on the War-time Elections Act 1917, see ibid., p. 139.
25. Ibid., p. 39.
26. Skelton, *Life and Letters of Sir Wilfrid Laurier*, I: 411.
27. Beck, *Pendulum of Power*, p. 223.
28. Ibid., p. 261.
29. Ibid., p. 50.
30. Ibid., p. 152.

31. Neatby, *The Lonely Heights*, pp. 61, 322.
32. W. Buckingham and G. W. Ross, *The Hon. Alexander Mackenzie* (New York: Greenwood Press, 1969), pp. 500-1.
33. Ibid., p. 501.

Index